INTEGRITY, COURAGE, & SOUL

Alvin W. Holst, Ph.D.

INTEGRITY
COURAGE and SOUL:

Leadership Traits for the 21st Century

Alvin W. Holst, Ph. D.

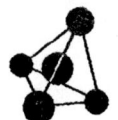

Integrity, Courage & Soul:
Leadership Traits for the 21st Century

Copyright © 1999
First Printing 1999

All rights reserved. No part of this book may be reproduced in any form, except for the inclusion of brief quotations in a review or article, without written permission from the author/publisher.

Published by: Alvin W. Holst
3023 Tomahawk Drive
Rapid City, SD 57702
(605-388-0050)

Cover by: Mark Hartman

ISBN: 0-7392-0256-1
Library of Congress Catalog Card Number: 99-94561

Printed in the USA by

MORRIS PUBLISHING
3212 East Highway 30 • Kearney, NE 68847 • 1-800-650-7888

TABLE OF CONTENTS

	Page
Table of Figures	vii
Acknowledgments	ix
Introduction	1

CHAPTER

Part One - The Importance of Integrity — 11

   1. The Unknown and Unexamined Life — 13

   2. A Dysfunctional Cultural Heritage — 25

   3. Negative Cultural Practices — 31

   4. The Closed System — 43

   5. The Nature and Function of Addiction — 63

Part Two - The Composite of Human Energy Sources — 73

   6. Integral Energy Components — 75

   7. Integrity as a Result of Putting it Together — 81

   8. A Theoretical Model of Integrity — 91

   9. The Open System — 103

Part Three - Achieving Integrity — 127

   10. Intellectual Power — 129

   11. Emotional Power — 145

   12. Physical Power — 159

   13. Moral Power — 169

   14. Spiritual Power — 181

Part Four - Achieving Life's Potential Through Integrity   191

    15. The Realization of Freedom.   193

    16. Paradigm Shift Revisited   203

    17. Exemplars of Human Integrity   213

    18. The Future for Integrity in the Face of Chaos   237

Epilogue   247

End Notes   251

Index   267

TABLE OF FIGURES

		Page
1.1	Time line - basic figure	22
3.1	Time line - negative cultural practices	32
4.1	Population growth curve - basic figure	47
4.2	Population growth curve - closed system	51
8.1	Theoretical model of integrity	98
9.1	Time line - positive cultural practices	106
9.2	Population growth curve - open system	116
13.1	Moral development curve	177
17.1	Orientation to relationship	221

Acknowledgments

My life has been a journey, in many respects very modest, since the only travel outside of the continental United States has been across the border between Arizona and Mexico and to the islands of Puerto Rico and St. Thomas. My journey has been very exciting within the confines of the continental US borders in that it has been essentially a journey of my soul. This journey has led me to meet many people both living and not living.

Because of my science background I am reminded of something Sir Isaac Newton said, "If I have seen further (than you and Descartes) it is by standing on the shoulders of Giants." I am constantly aware that my growth, insights, and discoveries are not only possible because of great scholars and scientists but especially possible because of the contact with thousands of adolescents. I am also aware that many public school employees have contributed to my development. College students - both undergraduate and graduate - over the past nineteen years have challenged my beliefs in helpful ways. These people not only gave me a medium in which to try out the ideas of great thinkers and scientists but a place - a laboratory of sorts - to test my own insights as well. To these people I am indebted and extremely thankful for their kind acceptance of what I am trying to do.

Thanks to Mike Walforth for his patient attention to my requests for detailed technical assistance in creating the figures. His talent and skill in photography and computer manipulation of the model of integrity have made an idea in my head into a visual representation for others to see.

Special appreciation and thanks are given to Gary Letchworth for his construction of a model from Styrofoam balls and dowels. His choice of colors adds more clarity to the actual visual model. This is the model which was photographed, and computer manipulated for the picture on the cover, and used in black and white throughout the book.

Thanks to my parents for not only loving each other in a way that resulted in my birth but for their efforts at setting me on a path with high moral standards. Thanks to my two older brothers, Roger and Kenneth for their efforts at supporting my parents in their efforts of raising me. A special thanks to my twin brother, or womb mate, Allen, who has always been within reaching distance and a soul mate. A special thanks to my sister Judy, who gave me experience in surrogate parenting, whether she wanted me to act like a parent or not. Our family was the first community I knew and it was a better family than either of my parents families. Our family was less dysfunctional than either sets of my grandparents families. For the effort that my parents put into raising us to be useful citizens, I am eternally thankful.

Thanks to five very special teachers; Marietta (Kingsbury) Brodsky - sixth grade, June Lyman - eleventh and twelfth grade social science, Cecil Haight - undergraduate biology instructor and advisor, Maeburn Huneycutt - biology professor and Masters advisor, and Howard Demeke - educational administration professor and Doctoral advisor. These five people all exemplify many of the attributes of people with integrity. They always made me feel I was important and what I was trying to do was important. They taught by example and were always encouraging.

A special thanks to my soul mate, dearest friend and wife, Ida. She accepted me as though I could do anything and encouraged me to do what I wanted to do. Her soul continues to always be available to my soul and I let my soul mingle with hers. We have lived an exciting life together over the past four decades. Out of our love for each other we were blessed with two daughters, Tandy and Wendy. They have made the real task of parenting a joy. We are now enjoying grandparenting two fine young boys, Levi and Colten, our grandsons. Sharing their joy and excitement of discovery and their zest for life is always very refreshing. All of the world's children are our best hope for a promising future.

I am thankful for being blessed with life and having sound family ties, good teachers, and the multitude of opportunities for sharing, as a teacher, what I have learned with several thousand people. I am grateful for the way people have accepted me, my ideas, and my efforts.

Introduction

This book represents the greater aspects of what I believe I have learned as a professional educator. My experiences include nine years as a junior high teacher of math and science, ten years as a junior high school administrator, two years as a district administrator for curriculum and instruction and fourteen years as a professor of education. The material contained herein is a significant representation of what I learned as a professional educator. I have included the key elements which have made a significant difference in my life and the lives of those with whom I have worked, both colleagues and students.

The book is divided into four parts which represent four aspects of the questions of integrity. The first part provides information to the reader on WHY integrity is important. The second part defines WHAT integrity is. The third part explains HOW it is possible for people to move to greater integrity. The fourth section describes the outcomes IF a person, and eventually a culture do achieve greater integrity. Divided in this manner, the book can be read from the point of greatest initial interest of the reader. It is recommended that it be read in its entirety, regardless of where the reader may begin. The book is an integration of information, discovered through readings, awareness gained through actual life experiences, and personal insights.

While I was in the final quarter of college preparation to be a teacher, I asked the Director of Student Teaching the question, "What does a teacher do to maintain discipline in the classroom?" At the time, this seemed a reasonable question. I had taken an extra year of undergraduate education to become a teacher. I knew there was a problem with this question almost as soon as I had asked it. The Director was hesitant in answering and I could see his larynx moving up and down. Everyone in the Seminar was intensely focused upon him as they too, must have been wondering about this matter. Finally his mouth opened and he said, "Well, that is something you'll have to figure out for yourself." He then went on to talk about something else. To this day, I remember the rage I felt as a result of his response. He was honest since we had not been taught anything about "maintaining discipline." My rage was the result of my own fear of not being able to maintain discipline, coupled with the fact that after five years of undergraduate education, it appeared as though no one had any advice on this most important issue of instruction.

I remember pledging to myself, that if I every "figured it out for myself," I would make sure to share it with others. After about the first three years of teaching, I found that seasoned educators had no better advice than the college instructor. At this point I began to experiment and try to change things by using what seemed to make sense, not being sure that it would work or if I would be allowed to do it. I found that most people did not know or seem to care what I was doing, as long as there were no problems in my classes.

I remember, as clear as if it was yesterday, one afternoon after the students had all cleared the building when I discovered I had been asking students to do things I did not enjoy looking at much less grading. I made a decision at that moment, that has redirected my life positively ever since. *I will never again ask anyone to submit to anything that I would not like to do.* It provided me, it seemed, with at least twice as much energy and enjoyment, and as a bonus, the students' behavior improved. This was encouragement enough for me to go further.

Thanks to the creation of the National Science Foundation and the funding which was made available to Science and Math teachers, I was able to receive eleven months of graduate education in Biology and Chemistry. This schooling was on the campus of the University of Mississippi from September, 1962 through August, 1963. This was the time of forced integration of "Ole Miss" with James Meredith enrolled amid rioting on the campus. Witnessing this incident and living through the aftermath was a defining moment in my life. This experience contributed more to my growth and development as a person and an educator than the Masters degree in

Biology and Chemistry. Many new insights about the meaning of life and the role of teachers came from this experience. The impact of this experience and some of the insights thus gained are detailed later in the body of the book.

Another choice I made, that is equally as vivid in my memory, is the day I discovered I had to stop trying to teach the subject until the students personal issues were addressed. A significant incident occurred with a class, of over 35 eighth grade students, that had lunch prior to coming to science class. They were nearly always in a constant turmoil and it would take nearly ten minutes to get them to focus on the lesson, or at least be quiet. They were very likable and energetic students, not bad in the sense of being malicious or mean spirited. On this day, I was lecturing (probably more like moralizing) them about their behavior. "You are thirteen years old. Are you going to still be acting like this ten years from now?"

Larry, a tall lanky boy with freckles and rusty colored hair (a handsome man in the making) asked a question. He said, "What is supposed to happen to a guy like me?" I said, "What do you mean, a guy like you?" His response left everyone stunned, but wiser, especially me. He said, "Two years ago my dad ran off with another woman and left my mother, my younger brother, and me, and a year ago my grandfather killed himself." The obvious message was he had lost his two most important male role models as he was entering adolescence.

No one spoke (it seemed like an eternity) for a moment or two. The out pouring of compassion from the other students to Larry filled the room and changed us all. There were no more incidents of unbridled bedlam in the class, the students seemed to have made a major leap in maturation. It became more evident to me, that what was going on, without direct adult involvement, had been student initiated denigration of one another and especially of those with significant personal life problems.

At this point I ventured further from the traditional and accepted approaches to teaching, and established a classroom guideline for acceptable student behavior. This single guideline was taught repeatedly as needed before the subject of science was taught. The guideline simply stated is, "No person has the right to make another person miserable nor enjoy another's misery." Whenever there was a violation of this guideline everything stopped and we had a lesson in how to treat other people. I have used this principle ever since, in all dimensions of my life. It wasn't until I was in the doctoral program that I recognized my own discovery as consistent with Kant's *categorical and practical imperatives*.[1] If it cannot be applied to all humans and it results in someone being used by another it is immoral and unethical.

There are many lesser incidents of awakening on my part which have resulted in significant improvements in the way to create a positive and healthy classroom environment. Soon after Postman and Weingartner's book *Teaching as a subversive activity*[2] was published I felt exonerated from any of my former clandestine behaviors, at trying to make classroom instruction not only safe and comfortable, but exceedingly more productive in the acquisition of the intended content. Not long after reading this book, I found Paulo Freire's book *Pedagogy of the oppressed.*[3]

After I learned that is was okay, as a teacher, to be a radical subversive, Freire's insights gave me a goal to work on as an educator. Freire's two major theses are, that those who live under oppression learn to be oppressors, and are better at oppression than those from whom they learned. Frankly, this insight left me somewhat demoralized and depressed for some time, maybe ten years. One day in my musing about how to change things for the better, it occurred to me to stand Freire's insight on its head, or at least the way I had been looking at it. In other words, those who live within systems of compassion, hope and love become compassionate, hopeful sources of love and they are better at it than those from whom they have learned. This cleared the fog in my mind and from there I set out to do just that, create a climate of compassion, hope and love in everything I do.

My experiences, by this time, had become a journey from which I could never turn away or give up.

It seemed that everywhere I looked I found more and more people writing and talking about things that made sense but there were still many gaps. In the summer of 1984 I attended a 5 day conference at Tarrytown, New York called *The coming explosion in education.* This was a significant emotional experience to be immersed in a community of around 500 people of my same orientation. When I returned to my campus teaching, I immediately and subversively, put in place, in my courses, principles I had heard of from Feurstein, Muller, McCarthy, Buzon, Samples, Howard Gardner, and Rico to name those in whose sessions I had participated.

Not too many months before this, I had been given a book to read by a colleague, one of many colleagues who have directed me to many readings. This particular book of Hutchins, *The conflict in a democracy*[4] made me aware that the responsibilities of the church, the school and the home are spiritual, intellectual or thinking and moral development respectively. Hutchins' observation was that conflict ensues when one of the three institutions attempts to assume the responsibility for one of the other or both. The conflict is the result of the rightful responsibility being neglected, and the unsuccessful usurpation of the others' authority without the commensurate expertise to assume the responsibility.

This was soon followed by hearing a local Medical Doctor, a general practitioner, talk about holistic medicine. Ray Strand, MD identified the holistic approach as including not only the physical but the emotional and spiritual aspects as well.[5] These ingredients from Hutchins and from holistic medicine provided a kind of primordial mix of information out of which, in an instant of insight, a theory of integrity became clear to me, in the middle of the night. I was awakened by this clear vision of what integrity might be.

I am sure my science background and the theories of the structure of matter led me to conceptualize a theoretical model of integrity, which resembles the atomic structure of the carbon atom; a tetrahedron or a triangular pyramid with four corners. Each corner of the tetrahedron represents the approximate location of an electron with the other two electrons deeper inside and surrounding the nucleus of the atom. In a flash of understanding, it seemed to make great sense that all humans have five sources of energy. The four corners of the tetrahedron are the physical, emotional, moral and intellectual sources of energy and the nucleus represents spiritual energy; all five are sources of energy to be developed as the basis for living soulfully and with courage. This model of integrity has been an important structure around which I have organized my understanding of the meaning of life since early in 1983.

It is my intent this book will not become so burdened with an air of academia, and therefore become distracting to the general reader, yet my effort is to ground it in enough of the accepted information, as to be a legitimate insight into how others can become empowered and empowering. This is a partial record of my own growth and development in the five energy sources and is therefore becomes somewhat biographical. However, it is not to be confused with an autobiography. Rather, it is my hope, people will read it and be able to shorten the amount of time for themselves, that it took me to arrive at these awarenesses. If people can acquire this level of development at the beginning or earlier in their adult lives, I am sure they will find their lives much more fulfilling, than otherwise could be expected.

I have used actual situations and changed the names of the real people involved. It has been my experience that putting people into the "story" increases the clarity of the intended message. My apologies are offered to anyone who may be embarrassed by being referred to through the use of fictitious names, in relating a situation involving them.

I am concerned that the youth of today have an underdeveloped soul and will become adults with very little soul. All youth have a soul, but the lack of soulful development creates pain, which they try to get rid of by doing all of the things that adults of today see as problems. The confusion is in large part due to the fact youth see adults doing these same things, and equate it with being adult and having power. The adults generally do not see the real problem, the pain of the soul, so therefore they mistakenly think that gambling, vandalism, gangs, drugs, sex, thievery, murder, hot-rodding, and addictive behavior in general are the problems. Adults are calling the symptoms of *a soul in pain* a problem. Nothing significant will change, except get worse, until more adults realize that the problem is the pain of the soul; pain in the adults' souls as well as in the youths' souls. It is to this purpose this book is dedicated and offered as an aid for adults in becoming better stewards of their own souls as well as desirable models for our youths' soulful development.

Alvin W. Holst, Ph.D.
Professor Emeritus of Education
1999

PART ONE

THE IMPORTANCE OF INTEGRITY

"The life which is unexamined is not worth living." (Plato)

"Those who cannot remember the past are condemned to repeat it." (George Santayana)

"By the time a person has achieved years adequate for choosing a direction, the die is cast and the moment has long passed which determined the future." (Zelda Sayre Fitzgerald)

"There is a legend about a bird which sings just once in its life, more sweetly than any other creature on the face of the earth. From the moment it leaves the nest it searches for a thorn tree, and does not rest until it has found one. Then, singing among the savage branches, it impales itself upon the longest, sharpest spine. And, dying, it rises above its own agony to out-carol the lark and the nightingale. One superlative song, existence the price. But the whole world stills to listen, and God in His heaven smiles. For the best is only bought at cost of great pain. . . . Or so says the legend. (Colleen McCullogh)

Part One considers the possible answers to WHY? is an individual's integrity important. Individuals are created with potential to become more than many do in the course of their life times. This represents a tremendous un-tapped source of human potential. For those who will argue this is as it should be, and therefore, not a matter of serious concern, simply reflects their own sense of themselves. The concerns of those whose potential has not been realized endure greater pain, un-happiness, and a general sense of helplessness. It is my contention that anyone feeling a sense of powerlessness can benefit from a self-awareness of his or her potential. A person who can examine his or her fullest potential discovers strengths and develops abilities which lessen the sense of weakness. In fact, the person becomes more of what his or her potential already contains.

Ignorance contributes to enslavement and knowledge contributes to increased freedom. When people don't know they don't know, they are at considerable risk of contributing to their enslavement. The person who doesn't know they have the power to refuse another's directives, usually agrees to allow the other to control his or her experiences and decisions. Truly integrated people know a great deal about themselves and hence about being human and are not easily misled to their own self-degradation. The power of personal integrity cannot be taken from anyone without their consent. They must be so well informed as to know when some unscrupulous person is trying to violate their integrity. The importance of integrity is knowing that one can successfully prevail against any of those forces which are deliberately calculated to rob one of his or her humanness.

Chapter One

The Unknown and Unexamined Life

A lack of self-knowledge is abundantly demonstrated in the American culture. An example is a recent television presentation by a major network on the problem of drugs among youth. This assembled group of parents and youth were on prime time TV, ostensibly to shed some light on the drug problem of youth. The popular news anchor, moderated and asked pointed questions of both parents and youth. Many of the parents had been drug users in the 60's and 70's and hoped their children would not be drug users. None of the people on camera, the moderator, parents, and youth, except for one girl, actually understood what the drug problem is all about. This young lady said that the reason she used drugs was because of pain. The topic of pain was never mentioned by anyone else nor was she asked for an explanation.

The concept of pain is foreign to people who are not in touch with themselves; so foreign they do not recognize it in themselves or in others. The consequence of this TV program was definitely of less value, than those who put it on the air, had hoped, because they were committing the same errors as those who have caused the so called drug problem. The problem is not drugs, but a culture in which people are unable or unwilling to feel pain and seek out the cause of this pain. A response to the causes of this pain would end the drug problem.

How did our culture arrive at this lack of self awareness? What are we, as a culture going to do about it? We, as a culture, have failed to ask the profound questions which will enlighten our senses and lead to real knowledge. By not asking the profound questions, a culture develops problems such as addictions. All social and cultural problems have their origins in the collective ignorance of the culture. As more and more people become less and less self aware the culture becomes more ignorant. Ignorance of self contributes to a lack of completeness or integrity of the individual. When individuals are thus afflicted, they have less courage and soul. Without integrity, courage, and a soul that is in pain, people are unable to manage their lives very well.

"What is the meaning of life?" is a question which often causes uneasiness for people. They display even more apprehension when it applies to the meaning of their own lives. I believe this is a symptom of a person's ignorance of his or her own humanness. Without an understanding of one's own humanness the person is not connected to, or able to be in harmony with, his or her own potential. This condition makes it difficult, if not impossible, for the person to relate effectively with himself or herself. Not only is it difficult to relate with oneself but it is nearly impossible to recognize and effectively respond to the humanness of others. This uneasiness becomes an even greater detriment when the individual does not and will not seek to answer the question for themselves. Not seeking answers to the uniqueness of one's life adds to the difficulties of living.

This description of ignorance of one's humanness is intended to suggest an emptiness or void. I believe this is a major cause for the initial fear people have when thoughts of the meaning of life are considered. It was Thoreau who said, "Nothing is so much to be feared as fear."[1] Fear of the unknown cannot be resolved by either directly attacking it or denying it. Fear of the void can serve as a motivator or an invitation to examine the cause behind it. As a person discovers his or her humanness this emptiness disappears and the fear subsides.

Yet this is not what is commonly found. Some, and I believe a majority of people, develop ways to directly exploit the emptiness associated with fear in others as a means of external control or manipulation. Others, quite simply out of their own ignorance, address fear in others as a problem rather than as a symptom. The first approach is quite obvious, as being nothing short of parasitic. The last approach is less harmful at the outset but leads to the same sense of uneasiness in the fearful person. There seems to be no shortage of either type of ideology made available to individuals.

Some perpetrators of these various ideologies, vigorously seek to have their specific definitions adopted. This would not be a problem if the motivation behind this misguided and deceptive behavior was consistent with the true meaning of life.

The word *life* implies growth and development. Without knowing the traits of humanness some people openly choose to treat themselves and others as things or its. Without understanding the potential for growth these same people often see themselves and others as a means to an end. Organizations are frequently operated where workers are used as a means to a profit; spouses may use their mates for personal gratification and teachers may use students as a means for aggrandizement. This eventually leads to self-denigration, subjugation and exploitation of the ignorant. The common portrayals of a fulfilling and meaningful life frequently contain the seeds of stagnation and degeneration.

Discovering the meaning of life is a personal and intimate activity carried out in the company of others. The combination of ignorance of one's humanness and the intimacy required, render the individual totally vulnerable. All learning takes place at an intimate level. People who are forced or obliged to relate to others who are equally ignorant of the traits of humanness or are unscrupulous are soon exploited. This ill treatment is confusing to everyone. An unfortunate result, is for the exploited to conclude that to be intimate is not in their best interests. Stagnation and lack of growth then result.

All ideologies have historically been presented as the correct one. Many ideologies do contain elements of truth about humanness and they also contain falsities. Misleading definitions and explanations are often provided to the ignorant and unsuspecting. Often there is a lack of explanation, or the efforts to help the person find consistency are inadequate with what is known about being fully human. The lack of explanation and assistance is a serious problem. This problem is made worse by those cases where questioning is forbidden and not allowed. This condition leaves most individuals crippled or diseased. Crippled and diseased people spend most of their energy and power on managing their weakened condition. In some social, political and cultural settings this is recognized as both desirable and necessary for conformity.

Unquestioned obedience is striking in resemblance to unconsciousness. Living unconsciously further detracts from normal growth and development. The meaning of life is then defined (erroneously) as this condition or disease. Without the condition, the person fears that life will have no meaning, least of all one he or she can manage as well as the disease. The person has become fully indoctrinated into a crippling ideology as a substitute for the meaning of life. At this point people dutifully take the responsibility of perpetuating a cruel hoax against themselves in the name of meaningful living.

This tragic condition becomes more universal the more it is practiced. Another of Thoreau's insights, nearly a century and a half ago noted, "The mass of men lead lives of quiet desperation. What is called resignation is confirmed desperation."[2] David Reisman nearly a century later describes an eventual outcome of living a desperate life in his book *The Lonely Crowd*.[3] Reisman describes fully indoctrinated, inner-directed, people as living with the equivalent of gyroscopes installed in them, that propel them in a direction not of their choosing and possibly without including others in meaningful ways. These lives are certainly empty of the deeper meanings of life which are most certainly possible for all humans.

Humans were created without an instruction book on how to live and without a definition or explanation of the meaning of life. A longer and more arduous struggle can not be imagined for our species to solve than how to live and define life. Prior to civilization, over 10,000 years ago, life was probably more a matter of listening to the genetic messages present in our ancestors' DNA.[4] This genetically coded information provided the basis for creating new life and sustaining existing life. This provided very simple ways to carry out life's activities. Food was taken from what was available in the environment and shelter was taken where it could be found. New individuals were created as the two genders responded to their inner sexual impulses. The new person was carried along, living as a member of the group. This type of life may be hard for some to imagine today. For many, the thought of living this way is disgusting and possibly frightening.

I believe this lack of knowledge of the humble beginnings of humans, to a considerable degree, contributes to the continuation and intensification of the stagnation and degeneration that is so prevalent in today's world. Each generation receives the immediate genetic material from the previous generation. Therefore each must learn how to listen accurately to the instinctive messages. It is not clear whether there has been any significant genetic evolution of humans in the last ten thousand years, or if there has been, it is not well documented. The problem each generation inherits is acquiring a workable or manageable knowledge of its genetic messages.

People who are ignorant of the genetic programming of the human species suffer a significant handicap. They can not manage the next level of awareness or knowledge. Previous generations developed ways to pass on to the next generation that which benefited the culture. Once civilization got underway and people began to live less and less in isolation of each other, ways had to be developed to manage the new problems of socialization. Ignorance of genetic programming and knowledge of how previous generations succeeded and failed in managing growth and development must be overcome by each individual in every generation. Some form of rudimentary education is now required to overcome the ignorance with which each person is born.

Not knowing we do not know, both our genetic potential and the cultural rules of previous generations, is a significant obstacle. Indications are that the earliest efforts to bridge one generation to the next generation included at least an oral tradition of lore and knowledge. This attempt at education was seen as a way to accelerate the development of each new generation so the community could maintain the advantages gained in the previous generation. As culture became more complicated, it became necessary to make recordings outside of the body. These written accounts of data created a necessity to be able to read what had been recorded. It seems that every time people pushed on the frontiers of humanness new potential was revealed. The earliest recordings were in the body in the genetic codes followed by written records outside of the body. The rapidity with which civilization advanced was directly influenced by the discovery of new human potential.

Surely there must have been many groups of nomads who perished from their own lack of knowledge. Some civilizations disappeared completely because of a lack of understanding of the genetic codes and external knowledge. Those of us who have survived because of the collective wisdom of our ancestors are faced with the same problems but of a higher order. It is Einstein who is credited with saying, "We can't solve problems by using the same kind of thinking we used when we created it."[5] One of the traits of humanness is that of rationality, the ability to think, reflect and function consistent with the nature of all life.

Figure 1.1 is a simple diagram used in discussing issues of time and decisions that can be either positive or negative. When the decisions are positive they are in harmony with humanness. The negative area, below the line, represents the area where many failed ideologies have wandered. A negative choice is to decide that symptoms are the problem. When this occurs effort goes into getting rid of the symptom. The positive, and hence honest, choice is to identify the problem and provide what is needed. A case in point is the so-called drug problem of youth. Drugs typically are not a problem to youth. They play with drugs or abuse them because they have a problem. I believe part of the problem is ignorance of the beauty of their own humanity. They believe they are not enough or they do not feel good enough so they take on what adults offer them, addiction instead of spontaneity.

Cultural and social evolution appear in the thoughts and behaviors of each generation. When people began to give up total reliance upon their genetic coding, they began to develop cultural rules and guidelines for greater harmony and success. I believe the invention of

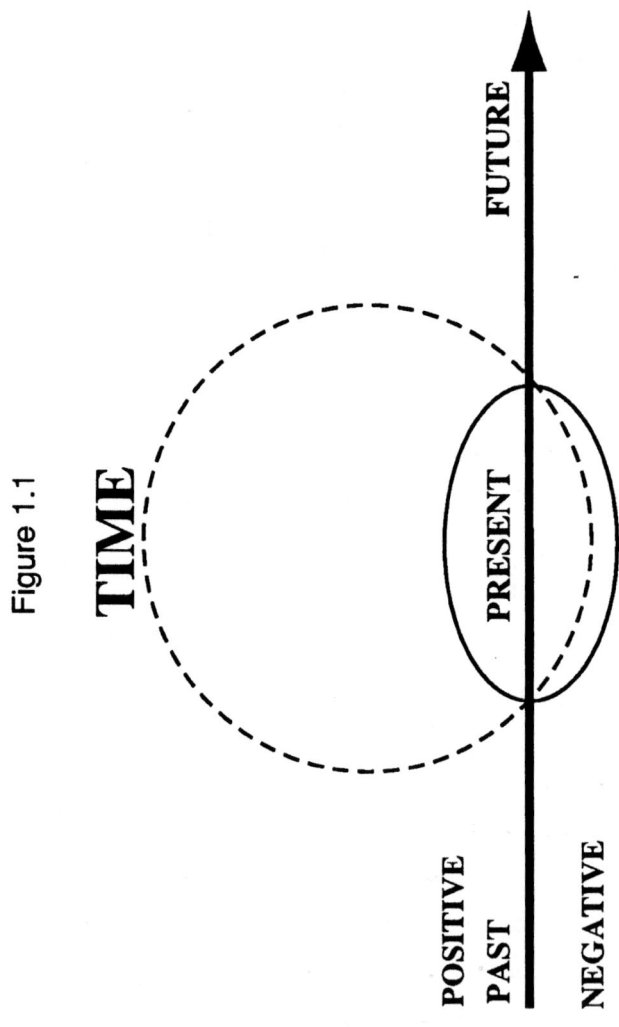

Figure 1.1

the concept of time in the western world has not been without its problems. Before the invention of time, people probably lived mostly, if not entirely in the present. This I believe is why children seem to be so happy in childhood. Once people developed symbols and language, they began to remember the past and anticipate the future. Choices that rely upon beliefs that the past and future can be controlled are erroneous. People are alive only in the present. Yet there are untold examples of people trying to control the past and future from the position of the present.

Sometime between 2500 to 3000 years ago some people in the Greek culture began to express concerns about the direction some of their choices were leading them. The question of good and bad or right and wrong began to be a concern. The conscious thinkers suggested people have the ability to choose good over bad and do the right thing instead of the wrong thing. This was seen as a human potential. Plato recorded his ideas in a description of the model city in *The Republic.*[6] Matters of ethics and morals were suggested as well as prescriptions for rearing and educating children. However, the Greek society in Athens was not totally positive, as slavery was practiced, in spite of the enlightened ideas of how to be more fully human.

The western world has been dramatically influenced by Greek thinkers of that time. Children were to be treated kindly and start formal schooling by age six. A person was to be at least thirty-five years of age to hold public and political office. In modern America children enter first grade at age six. The president of the United States must be at least thirty-five years of age. Ignorance of these cultural rules is obviously not damaging. Conversely, knowing about them does not seem to necessarily add any great advantage either. However knowing about these ancient cultural prescriptions for living, can give a person a deeper understanding of what his or her ancestors decided was an advantage. If the ancestors were close to what it is to be a human, the rules are what they were intended to be, facilitative. When the rules were off the mark or in contradiction of what it is to be human this causes the greatest concern when they are stringently followed.

Each person represents a composite of his or her ancestral genetic and cultural history. A lack of knowledge of either or both is problematic, if not life threatening. Each person must create his or her culture anew. It is a mistake to believe that this can happen through some form of indoctrination anymore than it can happen by mere chance. Education that leads to new levels of integrity and personal power offers a promising way for a person to navigate the choppy waters of creating a meaningful life and therefore finding a truer meaning of life.

Chapter Two

A Dysfunctional Cultural Heritage

Living the unexamined life described in the previous chapter allows people to perpetuate the cultural heritage for good or bad. This becomes a serious problem to the extent the culture contains prescriptions which are dysfunctional. A person can be unaware of human potential, as well as, the cultural prescriptions or habitual patterns of response. This ignorance of self and the cultural heritage leads to a robotic type of life. A life lived responding to unknown genetic and cultural programming can be dysfunctional, especially if the culture of origin was dysfunctional. Dysfunctional, as a term, is used in the context that the person does not progress in the development of inherent potential and may engage in activities which negatively impact the person and the culture.

Scientific evidence indicates modern humans reflect an ancestral past of at least 3.5 million years. This span of time, although very recent in the history of the Universe, has not been without opportunities to learn what it means to be human. However, the entire life span of humans occurred without benefit of any formal instructions, only what individuals have deduced from personal experience. The whole experience of trial and error provides the nearest thing to instructions. Trial and error becomes the teacher and the learning which takes place, in one generation, can be taught to the next generation without the risks of trial and error. In view of this delicate and dangerous practice, humans have demonstrated a remarkable ability not only to survive, but increase dramatically in numbers. The continual increase in the human population has been accompanied by both catastrophe at times, and profound benefit, at other times. People can learn from calamity not to repeat those things which may have caused the damage and then not pass them on to the next generation. When lack of attention to passing on the cultural wisdom occurs, it becomes necessary for succeeding generations to relearn these important survival skills.

Myths exist in all cultures and represent common themes among all humans. The existence of myths in cultures indicates attempts at dealing with problems when the truth or reality was not yet known. Joseph Campbell, in discussing myths associated with divinity, with Bill Moyers, said, "The influence of the dominant divinity in my mind will be what determines my decision. If my guiding divinity is brutal, my decision will be brutal, as well."[1] When the myths come close to the truth, little exacerbation of conditions occurs. However, when myths do not accurately reflect reality, the problem plainly gets worse. Either type of myth causes problems when it is culturally transmitted with the message, "do not question or examine." It is this taboo of not questioning the cultural messages, which contributes to the cultural dysfunction.

The rationale for not questioning the folkways and mores of the culture are encouraged as a means to maintain "stability" from generation to generation. This is of great value when the messages are congruent with what it means to be human. The destructive aspects of the transmission of flawed or inaccurate messages, causes the dysfunction and the misery within the culture. The Western cultures have repeated many of the dysfunctions which they tried to escape by coming to the North American continent.

The Puritans sought freedom to worship God as they chose but were quick to set up an authoritarian culture, probably more oppressive and dysfunctional than the one from which they fled. These early settlers on the North American continent, as well as later immigrants, eventually developed a plan for the extinction of the indigenous people already living here. A whole set of beliefs were developed to justify the extinction. The practice of slavery in the United States is another example of the exploitation of one group of people for the advantage of others. The Quakers were able to see the error of slavery and one hundred years before the Civil War, no Quaker held slaves. Some of the bloodiest riots in the history of the United States occurred as the result of making the Protestant schools into public schools as a method of curtailing or inhibiting the development of the Roman Catholic faith in the United States.[2]

Paulo Freire, a Brazilian, observed that people who live under oppression learn to be oppressors.[3] These new generations of oppressors are more skilled at oppression than those from whom they learned. This is a critical observation of the twentieth century which is beginning to be taught in some colleges and universities. The myths of the culture all need reexamining for two reasons: first, it is necessary to check them for truth and goodness, and second, if they are truthful and good, they are then owned or internalized by the person who checked them for truthfulness. If the myths are found to be false and bad they can be discarded.

Challenging the appropriateness or truth of the cultural beliefs is no small undertaking, in view of the weight brought to bear on those who would do so, and therefore possibly, alter the culture. Altering the culture historically has been considered bad and not to be tolerated. Attempts at correcting the flawed myths and beliefs has typically been labeled as treason and/or heresy, and therefore, punishable at the hands of those in authority.

Although not as common today as in generations past, those in authority have maintained their positions of authority through the practice of hate. Yet, no one holding a responsible position of authority would openly state they were acting out of hate. Still, groups of people have belonged and still belong to the Ku Klux Klan, Aryan Nation and Free Separatists. The focus of their hate is very clear in word and deed. The major flaw is as much the hate, as it is the blindness which binds them to their cause.

The blindness is nothing less than ignorance of that which they hate, which is really an extension of themselves. This ignorance of self has the effect of making them feel powerless. Rather than look within and alleviate the ignorance, they believe the cause is outside of them in the society. The focus is then upon a certain segment of the population. The group may be identified as members of a specific race, religion or political ideology.

Eric Hoffer very clearly identifies those who choose to hate as fanatics and gives them the name, *The True Believers*.[4] His definition of fanatics are people who find something to hate and then devote their lives to ridding society of this imagined devil. The paradox of this approach has two decidedly negative aspects: first, fanatics are never involved in building up anything only tearing down and second, should they succeed (and the devil is eliminated) their lives are suddenly empty of meaning. The fanatics' imagined devil has controlled them all of the time.

The post Cold War days reveal much searching, by many in America, for a new devil, since nearly everyone alive was encouraged to help destroy Communism.

President Reagan declared Moscow the seat of evil in the world, which appealed to a supportive electorate. Much of the turbulence in the United States, and maybe the world, for that matter, is now due to the loss of the "patriotic" cause of defeating the devil of Communism. Some prospects have surfaced as replacements such as dealers of illegal drugs, homosexuals, illegal aliens, African Americans, Catholics, Jews, Latinos, Native Americans, and again most recently, Asians. A student, in a junior high school, in which I worked has written letters to a local newspaper editor denouncing the Jews as the cause of the financial problems in the world. This hatred of the Jews was espoused while he was serving time in a Federal prison for his unhealthy and illegal practices in marketing meat products.

Belaboring the point of dysfunctionality within the culture by sighting an endless list of examples, will not serve to enlighten the reader much more than the preceding paragraphs. Yet, it is important to galvanize a sense of alertness in the individual that they are more than likely doing things, either by commission or omission, which can prolong the dysfunction of people within society. The greatest contributor to dysfunction is a negative belief or attitudinal system. My experience has led me to conclude that most people believe they are more positive than they really are. Therefore the next issue, to be presented, is the practice of negativity in the culture.

Chapter Three

Negative Cultural Practices

The basic contributor to a dysfunctional culture has its origins in the negativity of thoughts and actions of the people. The awareness of the existence of cultural negativity and practices can encourage people to replace them with constructive thoughts and practices.

Returning to the figure presented in chapter one, it is possible to pin point some of the factors which are expressions of negativity within a culture. These have been placed below the line or shaft of the arrow, in Figure 3.1, and represent some of the many practices essentially negative to human growth needs.

Below the line are listed eight conditions which are negative and may inhibit the full realization of humanness. It is no wonder that many people feel so discouraged about being human and lament their circumstance by saying, "I'm only human." This list can be expanded, as it frequently has been during presentations to groups and college classes. For every negative factor that can be identified and located below the line, there is a corresponding positive factor that can be found, selected, and placed above the line.

This list begins with a negative attitudinal condition known as pessimism. Martin Seligman, in *Learned optimism*, describes pessimists as people who

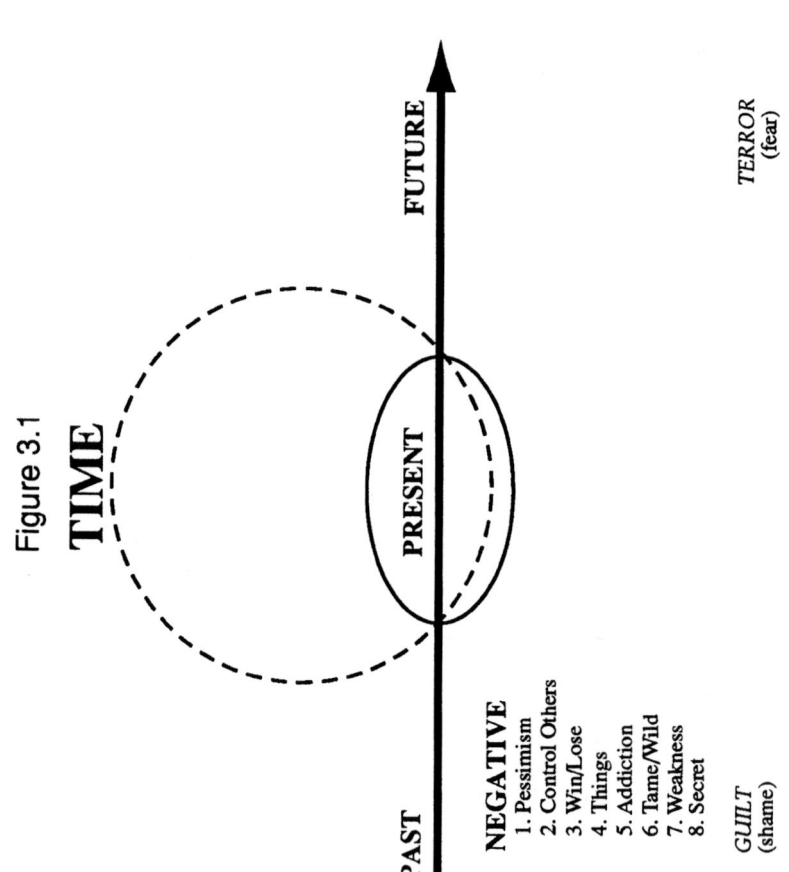

Figure 3.1

". . .believe bad events will last a long time, will undermine everything they do, and are their own fault."[1] The effects are reflected in pessimists giving up more easily and getting depressed more often. Seligman believes pessimism is learned, and therefore can be alleviated by learning optimism. The hallmark end-state of pessimism is depression, and Seligman calls the incidence of depression in the American culture an epidemic, with more people dying from depression than from AIDS.[2]

A measure of optimism/pessimism was developed by Seligman called the Attributional Style Questionnaire (ASQ).[3] My use of the ASQ has been helpful in preparing people to be teachers and administrators. Once a person has a measurement of their positiveness/negativeness, they are more able to resolve those issues of negativeness and become more optimistic. It is important to pay attention to beliefs and attitudes for they are the bases of behaviors. A person who acts positively but holds negative attitudes and beliefs, can not do so without eventually losing control and revealing the underlying negative attitudes.

The second entry under the negative heading, in Figure 3.1, is a predisposition to "control others". Controlling others is a negative behavior and implies that when a person feels out of control the solution is, "find someone who they can control." Obviously the outcome of this is certain to make everyone feel helpless. Youth learn this very early in their lives. One day I was observing a teacher when the teacher put a students name on the chalk board. This widely accepted theory is, "This action will maintain the teacher's control." The student, Jay, said to the teacher, "You really get off on this kind of stuff, don't you." Whereupon, the teacher put a check mark after the students name. Jay, said, "You really do get off on this stuff. Why don't you put two or three more checks after my name?" At that point it was obvious who had control of whom? The teacher was completely defeated. This is the classical win/lose situation.

Next on the list is the win/lose orientation to relationships. This is an erroneous belief, since to contribute to another's losing is to lose yourself and not win. A popular win/lose belief in the field of economics is scarcity, which provides an exclusionary force, thus producing losers. This leads to the practices of deliberately creating shortages of material goods in an effort to drive up prices. I know of an economist who believes money would have no value, if everyone had some.

A correlate in schools is the use of the bell-shaped curve to distribute the "scarce" resources of knowledge in such a way as to make winners and losers of students. Students dislike being placed in competition for this artificially created and managed shortage of knowledge. Many choose to simply not play this game of exclusion.

Many teachers and administrators bemoan the inevitable *grade inflation* when every student learns what it is the teacher or professor has said they should know upon completion of a particular course. These moaning teachers practice deceit and deception in order to produce a "normal distribution" on the bell curve. "Normal" implies winners and losers. Treating students as winners and losers is to act as though they are things.

The use of the bell curve was never intended to be used to sort people, only to describe a population.[4] This wrong-headed notion of grade inflation can be discarded in favor of teaching for mastery for all students in every class. The practice of honesty in testing students only over what they have learned, without "trick questions" or questions over material that was never previously identified in the curriculum guide as a part of the course, is of critical importance.

To treat humans as "its" instead of "gifts," is to distance ones self from emotional connection to others. People who are treated as "its" feel like objects to be manipulated and exploited. This further contributes to a sense of a lack of control in one's life. It is devastating to never be taken seriously by someone who is important to you. There are many adages which the culture perpetuates for the purpose of treating humans as things. One of the less noble ones is "Children are to be seen and not heard." This emptiness which is experienced by the "losers," who are seen as things, leads to a serious cultural problem known as addiction. This topic is covered in greater depth in chapter 5. Addictions are substitutes for the things lacking in a person's life and go against reason. Youth engage in those things which are deemed wild and therefore need to be controlled or tamed.

The dualism of tame versus wild, listed as item 6 in Figure 3.1, has been a guiding principal for centuries. The implication is that wild is bad and tame is good. The closed system has justified the use of practices which ultimately include killing the "wild" people because they are "savages" and therefore defective. Being of a different culture has typically been seen as not only wild but having an inherent weakness. In the minds of those who think and act negatively, "It is this weakness which must be eradicated."

People who are caught up in promoting negativity within the culture, seek out others' flaws or weaknesses and then relate to the weakness and not the person. The term "bastard" used to describe the birth of a child whose father and mother were not married, is an egregious example of weakness identity. The child had no real say in whether his parents were married, but is labeled for life. Much of what passes for sound educational testing practices in schools ends up being little more than looking for weaknesses, attributed to the weakness of the child. Children know how to learn in more ways than anyone knows how to teach them. Because someone has not figured out how to teach them, this somehow becomes the childrens' fault.

A young woman, Betsy, explained to me, shortly before she went out to do the student teaching experience, that she didn't know how she was going to handle how people reacted to her condition. Betsy had Juvenile Rheumatoid Arthritis and was noticeably limited in her walking ability. She explained to me, through tear filled eyes, what her fear was. She said, "All my life, whenever I am sitting down, people relate to me the way I like them to, but as soon as I stand and start to walk, they relate to my disease. I feel so helpless."

Around negative people, those who are struggling to overcome the limitations imposed by negative thinking often are attacked for being different. "They are too nice to be a teacher," "They have been to college and are bookish and think they know everything," "They are idealists and too theoretical and philosophical," and "They do too much thinking." The implications are that strengths are being mean, having little education, tolerating reality, and not thinking.

When a person is into relating to others through weakness they will try to make the person's strengths into weaknesses. Caroline Myss calls this "woundology", one person reveals his or her wounds or weaknesses and the other reciprocates and this is the bond for what is intended to be a friendship.[5] Relationships built upon relating to weakness and wound are not stable relationships. Between these associates there is a sense of mutual respect and honor of the other's weakness and it is to be kept in strictest confidence. Secrecy then becomes the force which holds these relationships together lest the one who divulges the weakness of the other be called a traitor. Secrecy is another way to control others.

The final entry on the list, in Figure 3.1, is secrecy. Secrecy is an illusion of the closed system in which many people have been mistakenly duped. Many things are private but never secrets, because inevitably more than one person knows about them. When the relationship begins to fail, as it inevitably will, there is a rush to reveal the other's secret to justify ending the relationship. "After all a person with this kind of flaw or weakness is really not a candidate for friendship for anyone." If the one ending the relationship can reveal the other's secret without giving a hint of his or her own weakness, then they believe they have won and the former friend has lost.

People living in this climate of negativity do not have a strong sense of the present. They spend the greatest share of their time in either or both the past and the future. Referring to Figure 3.1, the broken circle which passes through the arrow and the oval of the present, indicates a loss of a sense of the present moment. This happens because negativity contributes to controlling others and relies heavily upon the exploitation of a person's feelings of shame and fear. Both emotions, shame and fear, are necessary for the survival of the individual and the culture, since they guide a person's actions. Authority figures long ago discovered both emotions can be exploited through the application of heavy doses of guilt and terror as indicated in the lower corners of Figure 3.1. The difference between *GUILT*/shame and *TERROR*/fear is *PUBLIC/EXTERNAL*::private/internal. More is presented in chapter 11 on these emotions.

As a junior high school administrator, I have observed situations in many instances and discovered how endemic this reliance is upon the use of guilt and terror. First of all, I was expected to control youth, as I was the person responsible for student control. I soon found that the use of guilt and terror no longer worked as it had in the early 1960's. Youth refused to be scared or to be made to feel guilty. William Glasser in *Schools without failure* was one of the first to document this phenomenon as a cultural shift.[6] Later a very poignant scenario was to be repeatedly played out in my office which vividly revealed the inner workings of these controlling techniques.

The scenario usually began with a parent calling and telling the attendance clerk, a teenage daughter was absent and they needed to talk to the principal. The urgency of the call always resulted in an immediate conference with the parents and the daughter, Jennifer.

Invariably the father would begin by saying that, "Jennifer is pregnant. What suggestions do you have for us?" This emotional ice breaking was almost always followed by a predictable behavior of the father. He would turn to Jennifer and say, "You have disgraced the family and ruined our family name." At this point there was usually some discussion of what alternatives were available. Jennifer was feeling about as bad as it is humanly possible to feel even before her father's laying the guilt on her. Her parents seemed unaware that she did not want to be pregnant and making her feel guilty only made her feel more remote from her parents than ever. Then, often it was the mother, who, feeling some relief and a sense of control at the prospect of a possible alternative, would turn to Jennifer and say, "If we can get you out of this mess this time, you better not do it again or we will disown you." Jennifer now has been even more traumatized by the terror at the prospect of being rejected for what she has done. Negativeness closes in on those least capable of understanding, in this case Jennifer, and makes matters worse. Jennifer has been dropped into guilt and terror and is not really alive in the present, and hardly able to function at all.

  In an effort to honestly help Jennifer, the parents would be encouraged to accept that she was pregnant. It was stressed that she would survive this calamity better if she knew they would always be there to help her learn to guide her choices in ways in which everyone would be more satisfied. More is discussed in chapter 9 on the subject of emotional power on how to be accepting and a source of hope.

Chapter Four

The Closed System

The ensuing discussion has to do with the degree or extent of openness within a culture. When the culture allows people new to it, to enter and others to leave and have freedom within it, the culture is open. A closed culture does not easily allow people to enter or leave nor have freedom within the culture. The feature of closedness probably provided a very necessary advantage for survival of the human species but now has negative aspects associated with it as displayed in Figure 3.1 in chapter three.

The literature contains ample evidence that without an understanding of the closed system and where it came from, not much improvement in the human condition is possible. Efforts to improve a dysfunctional society without knowing the sources of the dysfunction can and often, easily lead to greater dysfunctionality. The closed system is the major contributor to the cultural dysfunction present in society today.

The closed system was not part of the natural world. The natural world by its very nature is an open system and contains every possibility whether humans recognize the possibilities or not. An example of non-recognition is the use of the term "chaos."[1] Chaos is a word which more accurately describes the state of mind of the observer than of what is being observed. Ilya Prigogine in *Order out of chaos* shook the world of physical sciences with his discovery that the laws of thermodynamics are not as Newton had believed. For these efforts Prigogine was the recipient of the Nobel Prize in 1977 in Physics.

Science was created in the image of the closed system. In this way the natural world was to be taken apart without regard for putting it back together. Prigogine believes the old science was naive in the assumption there existed a direct connection between the description of the world and the world itself.[2] The description was only what humans made of it, not what the world really is.

Just as Aristotle's notion of the cosmos was replaced by Copernicus, so now Newtonian science is being replaced by a more open system science. All closed systems are doomed from the outset to give way to aspects of the open system. It is this impending shift which intensifies the appearance of what is called chaos. With the old paradigms of science the true open system of science cannot be seen because it all looks like a giant mess or simply confusion. The ultimate question is, "Does one decide that what is called reality (in this case chaos) is more true than what could be true?"

The case for the laws of thermodynamics was strongly defended by Blum in *Times arrow and evolution*.[3]

The second law is sometimes described as stating that all real processes occur with increases in *entropy*. Entropy is defined as a degradation of energy and matter to an ultimate point of inertness. Blum argues that the second law does not apply to living organisms.[4] This pessimistic position is typical of closed system reasoning. It is this order out of randomness or chaos that is now being more fully studied through the power of computers. Randomness or chaotic disturbances can be shown to be predictable in the study of fractals where a computer can run thousands of trials in short periods of time producing evidence of a pattern. This has, in effect, made possible, observations of patterns which would not be observable in one person's lifetime.

The closed system was, most probably, created by humans in an attempt to control the unexpected and maintain a survival advantage. The whole act of control is the key element of the closed system. Every time a control is put in place it cuts off some possibilities and limits any new efforts and allows only the "accepted" practices. The charge of blasphemy, against people seeing other possibilities in the cultural ideologies has resulted in many being, tortured and made to recant or endure lasting persecution or put to death.

Those who tamper with the existing beliefs within a culture have historically been suspect at best and killed at worst. This cultural mind set of closedness is the major detriment to improved comfort and development of the members of the culture. The trumped up charges of heresy against Galileo effectively ended the scientific revolution in southern Europe. Today the heliocentric theory of the sun and earth's movements is accepted but was rejected along with Galileo, the man, in the seventeenth century. Closedness of a culture determines who has the power and who will use the power, and in what ways.

Jonas Salk, one of the widely known scientists of the twentieth century discussed the survival of humans in *The survival of the wisest.*[5] Being a biological scientist he applied the population growth curve or sigmoid curve to his description of what is happening to humans' cultural evolution in the twentieth century.

Figure 4.1 depicts the population patterns of all known living systems. Any given species begins with a few individuals and remains this way for a period of time. This is indicated by the lower left end of the S curve. When things reach some kind of "ideal" environmental advantage the population literally explodes and increases dramatically as displayed by the diagonal sloping segment of the middle of the S curve. When the advantages which led to the population increase are exhausted or no longer adequate, or in the case of people who can learn to control the fertility or birth rate, the population levels off as depicted by the upper right end of the S curve. Since evidence has been found of human ancestors which date back over three and one-half million

INTEGRITY, COURAGE, & SOUL 47

Figure 4.1
POPULATION GROWTH CURVE
(Sigmoid Curve)

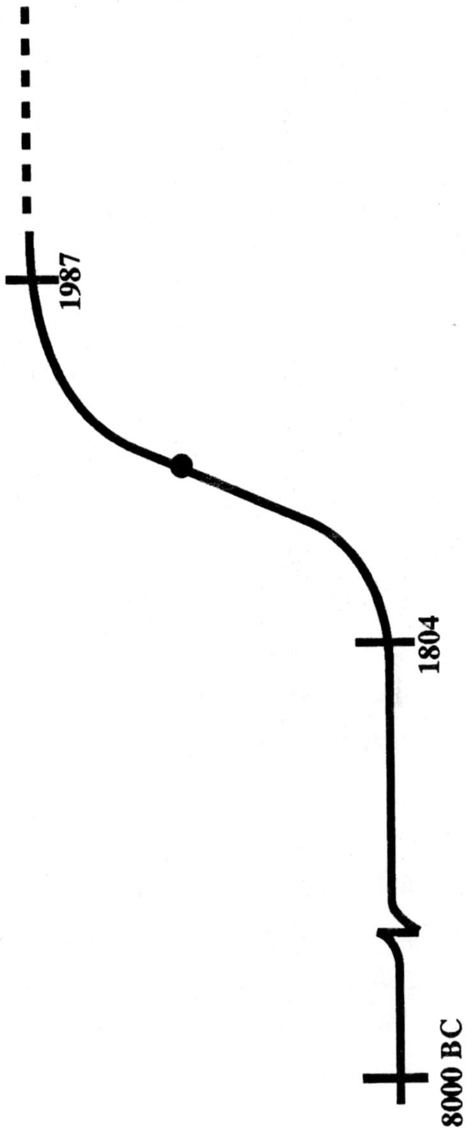

1987

1804

8000 BC

J. Salk

years, it follows that humans have had a long evolutionary journey. This journey set the stage for what has happened in the last ten millennia.

The sigmoid curve has been used in the study of just about every other species. Most other species pass through these population growth spurts repeatedly. Lemmings have always intrigued humans with their practice of periodically marching into the sea and drowning. This suggests a correcting mechanism within the species which prevents the population from exceeding the provisions of the environment. Many people have probably witnessed the cyclical population patterns of the indigenous plants and animals. Everything seems to have its season for proliferation only to be followed by a decline in population and another proliferation.

Humans, as a species, have never completed this cycle of population growth so therefore no living person has ever seen it in its entirety for the culture. It is reasonable to assume that a few individuals have achieved the fullest implications of this curve but their cultures have not. Figure 4.1 indicates what is reasonably certain of the human evolutionary journey. It took nearly 9,800 years after humans first began to domesticate plants in about 8000 BC and humans to reach a population of one billion in 1804. Five billion people were living in 1987 which is a five fold increase in a little less than two percent of the time it took for the first one billion people to appear.

Archeologists generally agree that nomadic ways of life began to give way to settled communities of farmers and herd keepers about ten thousand years ago.[6] Evidence of the earliest agricultural practices have been found between the Tigres and Euphrates rivers, along the Nile river in Egypt, the Indus river in India, and along the Yellow river in China that date back at least this far.[7]

The Department of International Economic and Social Affairs of the United Nations published, in 1992, population trends for the world, which exactly parallel what Salk indicated, in *Long-range world population projections: Two centuries of population growth.*[8] The human population probably first reached one billion near the beginning of the nineteenth century, 1804. And jumped to five billion by 1987. Some nations are showing declines in population however the world-wide rate is still on the increase.

The dot • mid-way on the diagonal section of the sigmoid curve is what Salk called the point of inflection. The significance of this point is very important from the standpoint of values. The lower end of the curve up to this point was developed by one set of values and the upper end of the curve requires another set of values to come into being. The cultural values of the lower end of the curve may have been necessary to the survival of the human species but those values seem to have negative and counter productive effects upon the advancement of the culture along the upper end of the curve. The set of values of the lower end of the sigmoid curve was all that Thomas Robert Malthus could see when he made his famous statement about populations in 1798; ". . .there was a tendency in nature for population to outstrip all possible means of subsistence."[9]   This undoubtedly promoted and expanded the exploitation of humans in the newly developing industrial work force. It should not be construed that all of the values of the lower curve are negative, however many of them are now oppressive. It is these oppressive and negative values which are to be considered.

Figure 4.2 reveals that from the year 8000 BC to 1804 AD represents humans efforts to have a more stable and predictable food supply than possible in the older nomadic life style. The concern for "food wealth" ushered in the paradigm called the "Agricultural Age." This paradigm shift has not been without strife and conflict among and between cultures. The nomads did not know the new paradigm, so acted on the values and principles of the older paradigm. Nomads were nomads because they had to be, to find food. The practice was to take food wherever it was found in nature. This was a troublesome matter for the new agricultural paradigm followers because it was often their herds and cultivated fields which were visited by the nomads. Some system had to be developed to defend the herds and fields from the raids of the nomads. This defense system resulted in conflicts between the two groups which are called wars.

INTEGRITY, COURAGE, & SOUL

Figure 4.2
POPULATION GROWTH CURVE
(Sigmoid Curve)

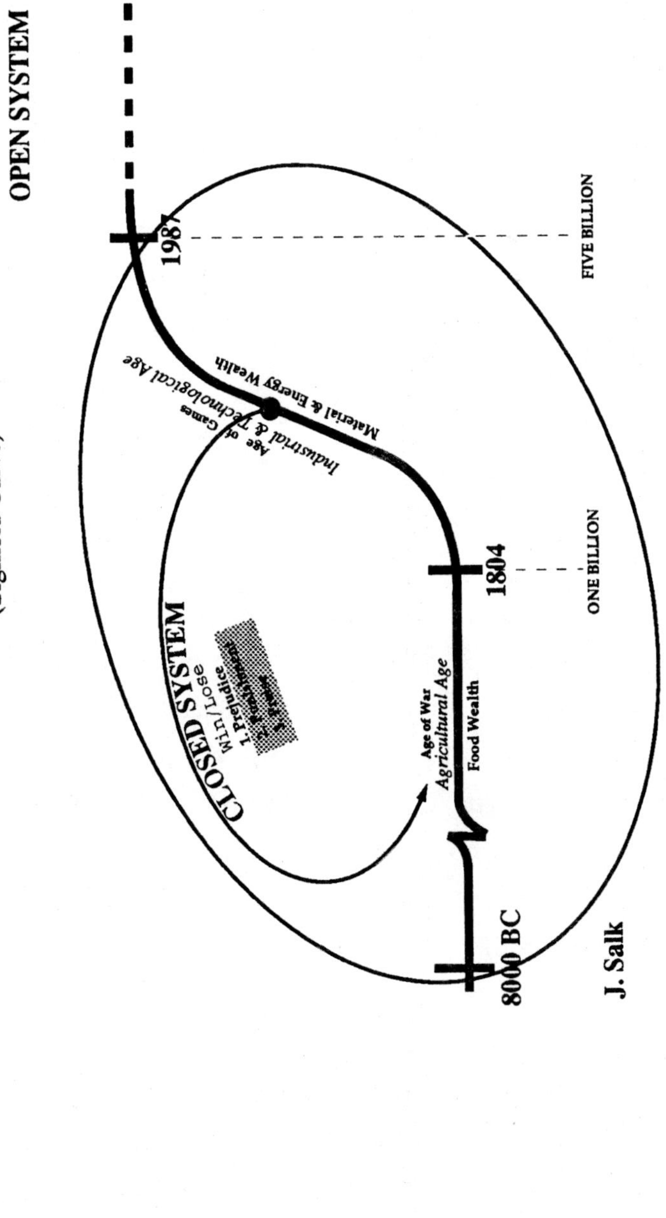

OPEN SYSTEM

CLOSED SYSTEM
Win/Lose
1. Prejudice

Age of War
Agricultural Age
Food Wealth

Age of Games
Industrial & Technological Age
Material & Energy Wealth

8000 BC — 1804 — 1987

ONE BILLION — FIVE BILLION

J. Salk

The initial problems were those associated with having increased food wealth which brought the two paradigms into conflict.

The agricultural age then became the age of war as a means of preserving the food supply necessary for survival. War was initially a hand to hand encounter with the more physically able individuals prevailing in their own interests. Humans understood the importance of defending the important resource of food. War was not always limited to securing a supply of food wealth and some cultures became warriors for the worst reasons, for the sake of human domination. The Lakota people of the west-central plains of the United States were the last major group of nomads to be defeated in war as marked by the Wounded Knee massacre in 1891. This represented a significant clash between the value systems and cultures of the agricultural settlers and nomadic Native people. Starvation was the major military tactic of the U.S. Government through the near eradication of the buffalo. The dominant culture of the United States not only had the advantage of food wealth but was beginning to share in the advantages of the next major paradigm shift.

The industrial and technological age had already begun in Europe with the invention of the steam engine and was gaining momentum in the United States by the beginning of the nineteenth century. The success of the agricultural age had contributed to the appearance of one billion people for the first time in human history. The fledgling nation of America had not only been a fertile continent for the agricultural and industrial/ technological paradigms but for the ideas of democracy. The ideas of inalienable rights such as life, liberty and the pursuit of happiness found acceptance in America. War was now believed to be obsolete and a nation only needed to defend itself from invasion. The location of the capital of this new nation, Washington, D.C., was located on a hill overlooking the Potomac river as a beacon to the world of a new way of life without war as a result of a new form of government.

A major conflict occurred over the issue of whether the nation should remain an agricultural based economy as found in the Southern states or move into the industrial/technological based economy of the Northern states. It was settled with one of the bloodiest of Civil Wars in the 1860's.

The conflict between the two beliefs or value systems was accompanied by the development of what is still considered truly American. The invention of baseball as a game in the 1830's and the development of the first rules of the game during the Civil War by General Doubleday. In the late 1860's, after the Civil War, the game of football was invented as a way to spend leisure time in the cool brisk weather of the fall the same as baseball was a way to spend leisure time during the "dog days" of the hot summer. Finally the game of basketball was invented in the late 1890's to consume leisure time indoors during the cold winter months. The problem of leisure time was an outcome of the industrial/technological shift since people were not required to work from sun up until sundown to produce food. Since it still took about 95 percent of the population to produce food and five percent to produce material and energy wealth at the end of the nineteenth century, leisure time was not that much of a problem. It should be noted that only men had leisure time as women still had 24 hour responsibilities as spouses and mothers.

Food production was still requiring about 65 percent of the American population in 1941, and when World War II was over, four years later, it took only about 35 percent of population to produce food. This was a huge cultural change. In effect, the war efforts, first developed as a defensive measure in the agricultural age, had become a tool for acquisition of material and energy wealth and this new wealth was used to wage war. Whether the United States as a culture has every recovered from this abrupt shift of paradigms is unclear.

The reader's attention is directed back to Figure 4.2 and the dot mid way on the diagonal portion of the sigmoid curve. From this dot a curving arrow points back to the age of war. This is the result of the peoples' reaction to the conflict of values in the two systems. The Vietnam war strongly suggested the futility of using war as a means to settle disputes. The civil demonstrations in the 1960's and 70's against U. S. involvement in the Vietnam war left people bewildered as to what is to be done. The United States had not prevailed in Vietnam although people were assured by President Johnson that we could fight and win a war at the same time we continued to develop as a democratic society.

Although President Nixon ended the active involvement of US troops in Vietnam he left office in disgrace as the first President to resign from office. The country was looking for a new kind of leadership and elected Jimmy Carter to be President. His efforts were largely in the direction of bringing peace to the world. One of his greatest accomplishments was the Camp David Accords, getting the Arabs and Jews to agree to preliminary peace provisions. The cultural wish for some kind of "face saving" over the failures associated with Vietnam was still simmering. President Reagan was elected because he promised to challenge communism at the seat of evil in Moscow and would not negotiate from weakness. This rhetoric of military strength led to the greatest military build up in the history of the world at a tremendous expense to the American public. The military expenditures expanded almost threefold during President Reagan's two terms. While the military budget was expanding the domestic human services budget was being reduced.[10] The rationale of that era was, "It is more important to prepare to kill people in foreign countries than to assure the appropriate development of America's citizens".

This military response from the United States is represented by the backward turning arrow from the point of inflection as shown in Figure 4.2. The new value system, associated with the next paradigm shift, was not as acceptable as the known value system of the past. This is a classic example of what Jonas Salk suggested happens when the values of these two curves come in conflict and people lack the courage to move in the natural evolutionary direction of human and cultural development.

Although there are positives to be found in both the agricultural and industrial/technological ages, to not move on, as has happened historically in the past, shows a lack of wisdom as well as courage. As shown by the selected terminology in Figure 4.2, the closed system is a win/lose system driven primarily by three practices. The closed system is the same thing as the negative orientation depicted in Figure 3.1.

The first practice of the closed system is prejudice. Gordon Allport defined prejudice as the willingness to believe anything which is false and negative.[11] Chapter three relates much of what is negative in a culture and much of it is based on untruths and half-truths all of which are an integral part of prejudice.

Although Allport listed five steps to achieving the ultimate ends of prejudice, I have taken the liberty to add one more, which is believing. Prejudice begins with **believing** - negative and false ideas which are followed by **talking** about these beliefs. It is not difficult to detect prejudice by listening to what people talk about. People have developed a language to describe everything they dislike or do not know much about. When people believe and talk about their prejudices the next steps are doing something overt or taking action which is observable. The first of these is **avoiding** who or whatever it may be they hold negative and false beliefs about. This is evident when someone moves to the other side of the street or mall so as not to come face to face with someone they hold prejudices about. When teachers have prejudices about students they avoid them by not recognizing them or calling on them in class.

The fourth step of prejudice is **excluding** those for whom prejudices are held. Women were excluded from the U.S. Constitution which resulted in years of struggle to win the right of suffrage in the 19th Amendment. Women have been thought of as property, which is negative and false. Students are often sent out of classrooms by teachers because of negative and false beliefs about the student such as, "every class has at least one trouble maker." Or as I was told as a candidate for a Master's degree, when I asked for help in class, "We expected to get a few people like you in the program." Exclusion or isolation of a person can be necessary to protect others and give the offender time to consider the gravity of his or her actions. There are appropriate reasons for suspension and expulsion of students from schools and these include intractable problems of unruliness and unwillingness to accept the appropriate decorum.

The fifth step of prejudice follows in sequence and is **assaulting** whatever or whomever the prejudice is directed toward. Slapping, kicking, and hitting are physical forms and yelling, intimidating, and degradation are verbal forms of assault. Usually the verbal forms precede the physical forms in application. An elementary teacher told a fourth grade student, "I know what is wrong with you, your mother was on drugs when she was carrying you. We should just put you in the dumpster with all the rest of the garbage. That is where you belong." Corporal punishment has long been used in schools as a way to settle the teachers' differences with unruly students. Many state legislatures have now made it illegal to assault students in any way.

The prejudiced person gets to step six by practicing and refining each of the five previous steps in consecutive order. It is impossible for a human to carry out step six without this preparation, since humans are not genetically encoded to engage in **killing** other humans. All of prejudice is a learned response to ones ignorance. The military has known this for sometime and uses "boot camp" as a way to prepare soldiers to kill the enemy. All kinds of derogatory names are invented to describe the object which is the focus of a prejudice. Each and every slur is offensive to the intended recipient and it is the rare person who has not been a target of someone's prejudice about them.

The second practice of the closed system is some system of punishment. The Old Testament verse from Exodus 21:23-25, "If any harm follows, then you shall give life for life, eye for eye, tooth for tooth, hand for hand, foot for foot, burn for burn, wound for wound, stripe for stripe."[12], makes clear the notion of retribution. This system of justice is a system which relies upon retribution also having a deterrent effect but the statistics of the 1980's and 90's clearly show otherwise. There are now more murders or capital crimes than before the law prohibiting capital punishment was overturned.

As a beginning junior high school administrator I paddled boys for the first year. Two things became very evident, their behavior became worse and I began to develop physical symptoms such as nausea. It is obvious to me that to do physical or verbal damage to another is to damage yourself also. I worked for nine more years, in challenging settings, as a junior high school administrator and never paddled another student. I would like to apologize to all of those students who I paddled in that first year. I am sorry and I acted out of ignorance.

The third practice of the closed system is one which raises many eyebrows and causes all kinds of semantic arguments. Praise has been shown by Mary

Budd Rowe[13] to be detrimental to student learning and is a large piece of Adlerian Psychology as developed by Dreikurs.[14] Praise is empty of information, it is judgmental of the person and is usually closely coupled to sarcasm. Junior high age youth, and older, do not enjoy, nor do they seek praise. When I have deliberately praised someone in a group, as a demonstration, the recipient of the praise relates a sense of discomfort. After some discussion it is easily shown the discomfort first comes from being singled out and they feel outside of the group and they also are unsure of why the praise was given. Children who are praised in class will often misbehave as a means to rejoin the group.

The practices of punishment and praise are highlighted to show the connection between them. Those with psychology backgrounds will recognize these as the hallmarks of "Behaviorism". The idea that all living things are guided by reward and punishment in their choices has been shown by Seligman to be misguided.[15] Reward and punishment are now recognized as the primary causes behind helplessness and depression.

There are other practices in the closed system which are negative besides prejudice, punishment and praise. However if only one of these three can be removed from a person's behavior, I suggest it be prejudice and the other two would disappear automatically. It is out of prejudice that hate comes. I would refer the reader to Eric Hoffer's book, *The true believer*, for his explanations of fanaticism and hatred are the most revealing.[16]

Chapter Five

The Nature and Function of Addiction

The presence of addiction in a culture is a symptom of the closedness of that culture. The more closed the functioning of a society, the less energy there is available for the growth and development of the individuals. This deprivation leads to a lack of development as all of the energy goes into controlling. I believe this is what Reisman described in the *Lonely crowd.*[1] An undeveloped person has essentially the prescriptions of the culture to guide his or her actions. Reisman describes this as having the equivalent of a gyroscope installed during the early developmental years. The person is aware of the lack of control of the direction his or her life is taking but feels helpless to do anything about it. The only alternative seems to be the adoption of some repetitive behavior to ease the momentary sense of pain from self-alienation. Alienation comes from not knowing one's self. The person alienated from him or her self is also alienated from everyone else. The depth of this alienation is felt as if the person is dead; not alive in the present moment. The American culture has historically offered many addictive alternatives for self-sedation. Youth try to knock out the effects of guilt and terror with an addiction, so they can have at least, a fleeting sense of the present and being alive.

I am reminded of a story about a dog that follows children to school to play during recess and play times. During the warmer times of the year, the dog lies waiting at the open classroom door for the children to go out to play. He holds a tattered tennis ball between his front feet and regularly grabs it with his mouth, in anticipation of a pleasure to which he has become addicted. On occasion he hears a dog bark in the distance, which reminds him of his ancestral connections. The dog momentarily looks in the direction of the bark only to remember the ball between his front legs and quickly returns to his habitual behaviors. The dog appears totally unable to respond to anything beyond the slavish habits he has learned. Everyone says he is a good dog but not good for much of anything.

To be stagnated and undeveloped is the outcome of living in a closed culture which prizes self-satisfaction at the cost of depriving others. Deprivation of others leads to deprivation for the one doing the depriving. Hence everyone feels less than fully functioning or capable. This deep sense of a lack of life within oneself is the basis for the quick fix approach to life's problems.

The solution to this problem is usually to find someone who has what you do not have and find a way to get it away from them. This was most eloquently and rhetorically asked of me by a respected professor of Economics at a flagship State University in his response to my editorial on the insanity of grade inflation. My position is that if everyone in a class masters the concepts and material they deserve a grade higher than a C. His question of me was, "Would money have any value if everyone had some?" His economic theory appears to rest heavily in the realm of the closed society. One's advantage is possible because someone is at a disadvantage. The logic of this theory always leads to a collapse of cultural moral fabric. One only has to look at the crime associated with the drug culture. This behavior suggests a belief that may be, "I'll have a more satisfying life if someone else is having a poorer life experience than me."

Major shifts in the cultural beliefs are called for here. Addiction is not a problem to those engaging in it! Addiction is the *solution*, although a poor one, offered to them by a culture which denies them the basic needs for healthy growth and development. This denial can either be deliberate or out of ignorance. Remember in a closed system another's ignorance may be an advantage for someone and therefore worth perpetuating to maintain the status quo.

Today in America youth are basically rearing themselves since adults display considerable dysfunction. William Golding describes in *The lord of the flies* what happens when pre-adolescents are left to manage their own affairs.[2] This story displays in graphic dimensions how earlier training of children can disappear when adults are not present to continue the lessons of civilized living. Golding described the theme of the *Lord of the flies* as, "The moral is that the shape of a society must depend on the ethical nature of the individual and not on any political system however apparently logical or respectable."[3] The moral or ethical base for a sound society must come from adults with considerable integrity. America's youth are in great need of more adults of higher integrity to model the known truths of the culture. Without this role model, youth are basically adrift in a sea of indifference. It should be no surprise that youth are joining gangs to fill the need of a sense of family. Unfortunately these surrogate families have adopted the same addictive solutions as the adults. Adults never become addicted, they become addicted during their youth and then move into adulthood as an addict.

During the span of time in which I worked as an educator several approaches were offered to curtail youth drug activity. The first efforts were "scare" tactics and since the use of terror doesn't work this approach was fruitless. A fifteen year old youth told me after one of these attempts at scaring them, "If you want to see something that will scare you, you should have been in my living room when my brother overdosed."

The next approach was to "educate" them so they could make the right choice. Officers of the law frequently instructed students, which included displaying large containers of confiscated drugs and paraphernalia. Often marijuana was burned in the classroom so the students would know how to recognize the odor. Telling students about drugs seemed only to increase their curiosity.

Another approach which became popular in the 1970's was to keep youth busy. A significant proliferation of youth activities, namely athletics, was tried. Little league baseball suddenly had a new purpose and expanded, girls softball was developed, youth football and soccer came later. The rationale seemed to be, "Keep them so busy they won't have time to mess around and if they have time they'll be too tired."

The approach of the 1980's was to teach youth to "Just say no!" which came from First Lady Nancy Reagan. This approach has continued with police departments getting involved and teaching youth Drug Awareness and Resistance Education, the "DARE" approach.

Undoubtedly some youth may have been influenced to not use drugs by these approaches. However the general trend continues to be more youth using more and stronger drugs. If one drug becomes more heavily used at one time it becomes less used by the next wave of youth only to be displaced by a different one.

The addiction of youth is not a hopeless situation. It is a difficult task to correct the causes behind addiction but not impossible. Much has been said about the power of peer pressure which seems more like an excuse to do nothing and an expression of helplessness. In working with students who have had drug problems, I have found two significant factors which do not get much consideration. Students in junior high schools have told me they first experimented with drugs the summer after they were in the fourth grade, which is about nine or ten years of age, and if it was not a member of the family who gave them the stuff, it was usually a close friend of the family. These are not peers but adults.

Children who enter the fourth grade typically experience a learning difficulty not of their making or due to any failure of neurological processes. According to Toepfer[4] and Epstein[5] the human brain does not grow linearly until adulthood is reached. But rather the brain grows in spurts separated by short periods of little or no growth, called plateaus. Their understanding is that while the brain is growing rapidly the typical left-brain curriculum of schools is easily learned. One of these plateaus in brain growth occurs at about age nine and what was easily learned before has become difficult. They suggest this is a time when consolidation of the previously learned curriculum takes place.

Recognition of the need for consolidation however is not reflected in the typical public school curriculum but a significant increase in the amount of left brain learning is thrust upon them. One example of this is the expectation they will learn as much in reading in the fourth grade as they did in grades one, two and three combined. These plateaus, it seems are an ideal time for right-brain learning to take place. And interestingly, the students who experimented with drugs after feeling helpless from the fourth grade experience often return to these drugs again at the next plateau which occurs at about thirteen years of age during the eighth grade.

The most insightful explanations of the nature of addiction comes from Stanton Peele. According to Peele addiction has the following characteristics: "it eradicates awareness, it hurts other involvements, it lowers self-esteem, it is not pleasurable, and it is predictable."[6] These are the hallmarks of the closed system. Peele further states the key terms in understanding addiction are "pain, anxiety, and fear."[7] Again these terms are symptoms of the closed system.

Peele uses addiction to gambling as an argument against classifying addiction as a disease.[8] The reason for calling addiction a disease is "it very usefully permits (those addicted to alcohol) to avoid the guilt drinking causes."[9] There are other arguments against addiction being a disease such as people giving up the addiction as frequently without professional help as with professional help. A friend of the family had drunk considerable alcohol until he was in his sixties when he quit. I asked him when he turned eighty how he did that. His answer was, "I thought I was put on earth to drink it up, but when I figured out they were making it faster than I could drink it, I said to hell with them, and quit drinking." He was "cured" by his own internal desire to have control in his life and avoid all the problems his drinking had been causing.

Peele's strongest position is expressed in *Diseasing of America: addiction treatment out of control.*[10] Peele's position is that treatment of addiction in the manner in which it is done actually makes things worse. This worsening of the situation is a ". . .paradox that as we expand our treatment facilities and public responsiveness we perceive our problems as less manageable. . ." and find ourselves relying more on something that is bringing less satisfaction.[11] This is typical of the addiction practices and of the closed system.

Not only is Peele recommending that we stop calling addictions diseases but as adults we need to change how we relate to children and youth.

> Instead of frightening children, what we must actually do to combat obesity and other addictions is to make our children less afraid and more capable of facing their environments, even though these can never be made fully secure and certain.[12]

Peele also points out that a primary purpose ". . .in taking drugs and drinking excessively is to eliminate the fears with which (people) cannot deal realistically."[13] The fears of not having control are only made worse by being addicted, since addiction takes control away from us. People who are obedient followers of the closed culture are accustomed to relying on external control so addiction replaces, in most cases, the external authority. The addiction is then the way the person gives external authority a place in his or her life when the controlling people are not immediately available to control them.

The only solution to the problems of modern American culture is to give up the addiction producing closed system practices. These practices are driven primarily by guilt and terror which deprive the person of a sense of the present. People will never experience the present unless they can escape the heavy cultural doses of guilt and fear. The premise of this book is that it is possible to be alive in the present and live with a greater sense of self-control and hopefulness.

PART TWO

THE COMPOSITE OF HUMAN ENERGY SOURCES

"All cruelty springs from weakness." (Lucius Annaeus Seneca)

"The strongest are those who renounce their own times and become a living part of those yet to come. The strongest and the rarest." (Milovan Djilas)

"It is the individual who is not interested in his fellow men who has the greatest difficulties in life and provides the greatest injury to others. It is from among such individuals that all human failures spring." (Alfred Adler)

"We cannot change anything unless we accept it. Condemnation does not liberate, it oppresses." (Carl Gustav Jung)

"It is only when we are misunderstood by others that we really understand ourselves." (Van Wyck Brooks)

Part Two considers the possible answers to WHAT? is personal integrity. The meaning of life takes on more significance when the individual becomes not just more complete but the blending of his or her energy sources liberates him or her from a strong sense of helplessness. Ignorance of the self is the primary factor to be alleviated in this process of integration of the self.

Synergy of energy of the individual leads to greater integrity and courage. This blending of energy from the five genetically endowed sources; physical, emotional, intellectual, moral and spiritual is the challenge of a life well lived. The quotes above are observations of a few from as far back as the first century well up into the twentieth century.

It is not sufficient for a person to simply recognize these as truisms, he or she must also replace his or her weakness with the requisite strength. Renouncing one's own practices involves giving up weakness as a way of relating to others. The misery of humans stems from not being interested in others and finds it source in not being interested in oneself. It is our own weakness which must be accepted, for to condemn another's weakness without correcting our own weakness is hypocritical. We all should welcome being misunderstood by others as they are telling us that we are incomplete in some way. A lack of integrity is the result of incompleteness. Remaining incomplete is to accept stagnation of one's own development and the consequences upon one's own integrity.

Chapter Six

Integral Energy Components

Every person is created with loci or centers of several energies. This sets up the potential for one's existence somewhere on a continuum of positive or negative. When a person is ignorant of the sources of energy within themselves they suffer a serious handicap. The more ignorant one is of his or her energy the more negative his or her experiences. This condition can be likened to placing an untrained person in control of a space vehicle powered by rockets. Without the required information, the flight would be reckless and ultimately a crashing failure. This is the way many people seem to live their lives. The violence in their lives is not due to a desire to live violently but rather it is the result of not knowing how to use their own gifts of energy or power.

Energy is the force which makes it possible for things to be done. Many people have written about how important it is for people to develop in several different ways. Usually they mention three or four and occasionally include some elements which are not primary sources of energy.

One of the most insightful works I have found is written by Robert Muller, *New Genesis: shaping a global spirituality.*[1] At the time this book was published Mr.

Muller had served over three decades in the United Nations, was then an Assistant Secretary-General in charge of economic and social services and coordination. During World War II he had been captured by the Nazis. He writes with some of the deepest and most compassionate understanding of what humans are facing. One of his significant truisms is, "You cannot expect the world to change before you change yourself."[2] I had the privilege of meeting and hearing him speak at the conference in Tarrytown, New York in the summer of 1984.

Muller suggests a core curriculum which he attributes to the former United Nations Secretary-General U Thant.[3] This suggests development in the areas of the physical, mental, moral and spiritual aspects of each person's life. This is an improvement over lists which mention only two or three of these energy sources and sometimes include social. Social is not appropriately included because it is not a source of energy or power but rather a manifestation of a person's use of the energy sources within them. A person weak in spiritual power, short on intellect, and immoral does not have effective social skills.

My conceptualization of a model of integrity was done about a year before discovering Muller's ideas. This conception came during a time of significant inner searching. I had resigned my position as a district level administrator in a public school district without a new position in sight. During the fall of 1982 and spring of 1983 I was on the job market extensively and always very close to a state of panic over the job prospects. Some time in March of 1983, in the middle of the night, I awoke with a vivid image of a model of how human energy is a part of human existence. Chapter seven details the exact structure of the model and how all energy sources are interrelated.

I am not entirely certain what influenced me the most in the conceptualization of this model of integrity. I am sure what I had been reading was the major contributor. The significant writings which contributed to this realization were from a book written by Robert Hutchins, *The conflict in a democracy*[4] and a talk given by Ray Strand, M.D.[5] on holistic medicine. Additional reading in the area of holistic medicine gave me deeper insights.

Hutchins explains that three institutions in a democracy have three distinct responsibilities due to their unique authority.[6] Schools are responsible for the development of the mental or intellect - *thinking skills*. Homes and families are responsible for the development of the moral or ethical - *decision making skills*. And the church is responsible for the development of the spiritual - *loving skills*. When any one of these institutions puts itself in the place of the other, it neither has the authority nor can it be responsible for the development of people. The rightful institution is displaced and its authority is pushed aside and therefore cannot be responsible in this situation. It is a very insightful look at what causes a democracy to deteriorate.

As an example, some religious groups take over the moral development and mental development and leave the spiritual development unattended. This example suggests why children who do not learn moral development from their parents and mental or thinking skills from teachers and are also left bereft of spiritual development. There is evidence that the Branch Davidians in Waco, Texas, are a recent example of what Hutchins was cautioning people about. The lack of spirituality is reflected in the expectation that followers would not make decisions nor question the reasons for things as they were. The enslavement of the person in the name of spirituality is not spiritual.

Holistic medicine as described by Strand and others suggests that healing of the body (the physical) is connected to both the emotional and the spiritual. The physical body cannot be healed with the best of the medical treatments unless the emotions and the spirit of the person are in reasonable health. As a matter of recent studies, it appears that when the emotions and spirit are not strong the person is more likely to become physically ill. Williams', *Anger kills*,[7] has found that people who are angry, that is emotionally upset, have a significantly higher likelihood of dying of heart disease. The explanation goes something like this, anger prepares a person to fight or flee an adversary. This is a necessary survival trait passed to us from the earliest of ancestors. However when the adversary is non existent in reality but imagined, the body, the heart and circulatory system specifically, prepare for the imagined threat. When this is a constant condition it takes a serious toll on the heart and circulatory system leading to lingering illness and premature death.

The reader will note the addition of the emotional to the sources of energy which brings the total to five sources. I think this is no accident that emotions or feelings have systematically been omitted. Descartes suggested that emotions and feelings are so unreliable they must therefore be discounted and ignored. For a thorough study and explanation the reader is referred to Antonio Damasio, *Descartes' error: emotion, reason, and the human brain.*[8] This mind set was adopted by the Western world at a great cost.

Daniel Goleman, in *Emotional intelligence,*[9] points out the dangers of not being emotionally intelligent. The person who rigidly follows Descartes' recommendation is essentially crippled. He or she can not effectively use his or her emotions as sources of information and therefore arrive at more prudent decisions. Not only is the person crippled by not having access to this energy, but probably the energy literally erupts in socially unacceptable ways. The emotionally ignorant person feels out of control, which he or she is, and therefore tends to try to gain some control by getting others more out of control. Aggressiveness usually springs from some sense of powerlessness. It is interesting to me to note here, that the person is not without the energy, but has never learned to recognize its presence and therefore does not know how to use it effectively. The details of how to use feelings and emotions effectively is covered in chapter 11.

Chapter Seven

Integrity as a Result of Putting it Together

As was discussed in chapter one, what has been called "pain of the soul" is due largely to the lack of adequate integrity. This condition is not something someone can objectively and rationally determine, especially during childhood and adolescence. The irony is that without integrity, one cannot readily know his or her degree of integrity. This condition of a lack of integrity is never-the-less felt by the individual as some kind of vague emptiness or incompleteness. The person is, as least at an intuitive level, aware of lacking something which is essential. This lack is essentially the same thing experienced when some important nutrient is missing from one's diet. The absence of Vitamin C in a person's diet leads to the disease or condition long known as scurvy. The same is true for a lack of growth in integrity, the person is weakened by the lack of development in these important energy factors. The person is not well put together and exhibits evidences of coming apart or disintegrating much as a lack of Vitamin C causes ones teeth to loosen and blood to seep into tissues and membranes. Scurvy is painful and a lack of integrity is painful because the soul is deprived of the energy of integrity.

In an open culture, the lack of full integrity, is not only a normal but a very desirable condition in an individual. It is this yearning to become whole or complete which moves people to explore and learn. Each person is in charge of completing themselves as a whole and integrated unit. It can be a joyous lifetime journey to discover who one is and fill in the voids. This developmental journey is rarely, if ever, successful without the assistance of others who have a greater measure of integrity. This is evident in the ideal parent-child, teacher-student, clergy-laity, medical professional-patient, and mentor-mentee relationships.

Children really have few options about who guides them in self development. In the recent past, much has been said about children and youth being "at risk." All people are born at risk. Yet the literature is full of all kinds of identified risk factors, which really don't matter. Living in rural areas, living in ghettos, being born to poor parents, being born of "mixed marriages", being born out of wedlock, having parents who use drugs or alcohol are all quickly identified as risk factors for children and youth. When a closer look is given to all of these listed and the many more that could be listed, it is easily seen that they all involve adults. So there is only one thing that puts children and youth at risk, that is the quality of the adult (how much integrity they have) with which the children or youth are forced or obliged to associate.

No one has ever selected their parents, or at least remembers selecting them. Children are usually sent to school to teachers they do not choose and go to religious training to teachers they do not choose. Children are therefore obligated or forced to associate with others, not of their choosing. This is of great concern when those they are forced or obligated to associate with are of low integrity. People of high integrity are very much alike one another when it comes to helping others in the process of self development and the results are quite similar. Good parenting produces good children, good teaching produces knowledgeable students and citizens, and spiritual leaders produce societal members with spirit and all three contribute to a well developed soul.

In chapter three the closed system was described as being the heart of the cultural practices which impede the development of people. The closed system is not open to helping others as much as it is into relating to others through weakness and punishing them for their transgressions. This is no where more evident than in schools. For the past two decades I have been having both experienced teachers and aspiring teachers brain storm for about three minutes. In groups of 3-5 they are to generate lists of all of the things they know that have been done to them, they have done to others, or they have seen someone do to another in the name of discipline. When these lists are posted on the wall and "force field analysis" is done, an interesting awareness comes clear to them. They have all made lists, with very few exceptions, of forms of punishment. Many say things like, "Only a person out of control would do those things. No wonder children are worse when they are treated this way. Teachers are taking educational practices and using them as clubs(*like writing a hundred sentences or detentions*). How did we get into this mess? How do we get out of this mess? What do we do instead?"

These findings have been consistently verified for nearly twenty years. Two things are of great concern, first, this practice of punishing instead of disciplining is endemic in our closed system and second, everyone has unknowingly and unwittingly learned it. There are few formal curricula that openly teach others (or would admit to this practice) to beat others up, humiliate them, and make losers out of them, yet nearly everyone learns how to punish. This is a problem of great social and cultural concern. How does one ignore the informal curriculum of abusing others and move to a new set of beliefs?

Two things are very apparent from this exercise. This is an endemic condition in our society and it can not be given up easily unless we know that it exists and we learn positive alternatives. The existing cultural mind set is very strongly in favor of lying about things and passing punishment off as discipline. The fact that the word *discipline* exists is an indication an earlier culture knew discipline meant teaching people what they do not know.

Punishment teaches only how to be punishing and that big people can hurt little people. The most detailed explanations of the differences between discipline and punishment are detailed by Bettelheim[1] and Dreikurs.[2] Dreikurs expanded upon Alfred Adler's theory that all human behavior has a purpose.[3] Understand the purpose of the behavior and the solution is readily apparent.

Many things go on in a school which effectively transmit the closed system and reflect this oppressive reliance upon punishment. Many people remember being humiliated in the presence of their peers, not allowed to go the toilet and consequently soiling themselves, then being punished again for soiling themselves, made to stand in front of the class and say they are stupid, made to run laps in physical education classes, writing sentences, standing with a nose in a circle on the chalkboard, sitting with a dunce cap on one's head, kept after school and harangued for bad behavior, hit, slapped, paddled, ears and hair pulled. The list goes on and on and the student behavior gets worse, especially when a substitute teacher is present. What energy a child has developed is not available to be used for additional growth but is now channeled into defending themselves and thinking of ways to get even. In many cases children give up on developing the integrity they will need to live a healthy and productive life for a life of defending and getting even.

There are many examples of the idiocy of the closed system practices but I will mention only two. Consider the student who has not learned to read and has a teacher who regularly asks students to read aloud in class. What choices does the student have? The student can try to read and then be ridiculed by his or her classmates or can start misbehaving before it is his or her turn to read. The misbehavior is the student's solution to his or her problem of not being a skilled reader. There is more face saving gained by being seen as a trouble maker than as being seen as stupid. Discipline requires that the student be taught to read rather than punished. The second example is the practice of repetitive chores such as writing sentences 100 times or copying the dictionary. I have asked many instrumental music teachers if they would keep a student after school and have them play one measure of the Star Spangled Banner 100 times. The immediate response has always been, "My God no, the student would quit band." Some teachers and parents understand this yet generally it is not widely seen as harmful as the music teachers see it.

One other example may help to make this point more clear. Suppose you are an outdoors type person and like to hunt game birds. You have acquired a well bred hunting dog as a pup. On the first outing the German Short Hair pup is eager to please and to do what genetically it has been bred to do. When the first bird rises on the wing, your first shot connects and the retriever heads off to get the bird, a small cotton-tail rabbit jumps up and runs. Let's say the retriever finds the rabbit more engaging and does not come back after you give your strongest commands. Only after you have retrieved the bird, does the dog come back, all excited about the romp after the cotton-tail. Hunters who love the sport and the use of dogs would not punish the dog by hitting him in the face with the dead bird. They know the dog would then avoid that with which he has been punished. Somehow or other our closed culture believes that children can overlook being punished and learn good by being treated badly, especially with educational practices, and then not object to the experience.

The schools are not the only institution where punishment is practiced in the name of discipline. Many children find themselves in homes where they must defend themselves and they also spend time and energy trying to get even. A paraphrase of what Freire[4] shared with the world, those who live under oppression learn to be oppressors and are better at it than those from whom they learned, is perpetuated. The domestic violence of today is the fruit of a closed system which is unaware of itself and is in a deep state of denial. Spousal and child abuse are at epidemic proportions and some children are killing their parents as well as some spouses killing their mates. These conditions exist due to a lack of integrity. Denial of abusiveness is the tip of the iceberg of dishonesty. Honesty in all cases is the foundational value of integrity.

The cultural movement toward "getting tough" on crime and criminals includes such shifts in emphasis as closing colleges and making them into minimum security prisons. This myopic view of human development is frightening in that if it is carried to completion, society has become a police state. Some communities have openly sought to become the sight of new minimum security prisons upon the premise of sound economics. Putting people in prison, for the sake of punishment, is never a sound economic practice. I first heard Juvenile Court Judge Gilliam of Denver, Colorado tell a group teachers, in 1961, that it cost as much to lock a youth up for one year as it would to send him to college, for four years, at any of the State's four year colleges.[5] I have lived and worked in four western states and in each of them this has always been the case and remains so today. A closed system not only wastes material wealth but more importantly it wastes the most important resource, its children and youth. And all in the name of sorting people into winners and losers. Keeping people in prison for long periods of time simply costs more money, and especially as the prisoner develops the health conditions associated with aging. And people in prison age faster than the general population.

On a major network, national TV evening news broadcast, I observed a newsperson interviewing a gun carrying, fifteen year old boy. The newsperson was moralizing the youth about the depravity of his ways and said, "Don't you know you could get shot and killed carrying a gun?" and the youth responded, "So. . ., I'm already dead." This is a classic example of the practice in our closed system society of essentially blaming youth for not being able to survive the depravity that society has heaped upon them. For a clear and more detailed picture of this general condition in the American culture I refer you to Jonathon Kozol's book, *Savage inequalities: children in American schools.*[6] One of the most reliable indicators of a closed system is denial turned to blaming the victim.

The open system does not blame those who are victimized but works to help them overcome their disadvantages. Blaming the victim is a typical behavior of the closed system as described by William Ryan in *Blaming the victim.*[7] The closed system reflects the reductionistic approach of taking the world apart and examining the parts in isolation of the other parts. Further, there is little evidence of any attempts at putting things together or integrating them. Integrity means putting the whole together so that each part knows all the parts and can function harmoniously as a whole. The closed system is destructive while the open system is constructive.

Chapter Eight

A Theoretical Model of Integrity

Any time a change in social or cultural practices is being suggested, it can be anticipated that some will ignore it, others will guffaw at it, still others will see it as a threat and attack it as well as the originator while a few will withhold judgment until the case has been presented. This is very similar to the responses to death as described in Kübler-Ross' book on *Death and dying*.[1] I first realized this sequence of responses when I was involved in negotiations with administrators and school board members over thirty years ago. Where Kübler-Ross identifies seven stages leading to acceptance, my observations led me to conclude they were four: denial, make a joke of it, resist at all costs, and eventually acceptance. I highly recommend Kübler-Ross' writings to those who want to go further in their understanding of acceptance of change.[2]

Another source of insight into theoretical propositions and human responses to these new theories or paradigms is found in *A Theory of cognitive dissonance* developed by Leon Festinger.[3] This is of particular importance at this point because Festinger identifies three responses with regard to contradicting evidence. The first is to dismiss it out of hand as biased and untrue and second is to accept this new evidence as correct and that we are wrong, thus making the new perception ours without question. The third response, which Festinger recommends, is to accept our original perception as how we wanted it to be, use the new perception as a basis for developing a new perception of how things could be closer to what we wish.

All of this brings focus to the point, that to change one's ideas or paradigms about a new belief or theory, or even about theory itself, is not easily done. Here it is helpful to call upon Thomas Kuhn's work on how scientists have historically altered their beliefs, theories and paradigms as detailed in *The structure of scientific revolutions.*[4] He points out, using historical incidents, that those in authority often find it difficult to change, - even impossible to see the needed change.

A mind trained in the closed system becomes a closed mind and either has difficulty seeing new ideas at best, or not seeing them at all, at worst. An excellent example of this was the problem Galileo encountered with the heliocentric theory of the solar system. During the seventeenth century the authorities placed the earth at the center of solar system, the geocentric theory, and would have nothing of Galileo's new theory. Even in the face of actual night-time observations, from the deck of a tower, and supported by mathematical calculations, the authorities could not allow the heliocentric theory to become accepted. He was found guilty of heresy and placed under house arrest for the remainder of his life. It was during the last quarter of the twentieth century that Galileo was absolved of the charge of heresy. There are many more examples from the twentieth century which could be used to make the point that it is difficult in many cases and not possible in some cases to see a new theory.

It is with this understanding that I present what I believe to be a new paradigm for the concept of integrity. To this point, integrity has been defined as being put together in a developmental way which allows a person to have ready access to all aspects of his or her power or energy. As was mentioned previously, this theory came to me at a time of considerable stress in my life, a time in which I needed more integrity. This time was in 1982-83 when I was without employment and heavily on the job market. I was entering the decade of the fifties in my life - a time I expected to provide greater stability. I had no idea the source of the stability, but being a male, I assumed it had something to do with having a job commensurate with my training and experience.

I believe the un-easiness for me had as much to do with a defining moment in my life from two decades earlier. I was on the campus of the University of Mississippi in 1962-63 through the financial support of the National Science Foundation to develop a greater background in science content. The Russians had sent up the first satellite in 1957 and the American response was to crank out more scientists. I was paid more per month to go to school than I was making in salary as a teacher.

I still remember that late Sunday evening in September 1962 when U.S. Marshals encircled the Lyceum building in preparation for the forced integration of "Ole Miss" by James Meredith. As a young family, over fifteen hundred miles from my roots in South Dakota, it was frightening to see what people would do when their belief system was under attack. The results of all night rioting with the loss of life and property, and the smell of tear gas is still vividly with me more than thirty five years later. I soon found out how much prejudice with which I had been raised, but I didn't know how to handle the prejudice of others directed toward me. I never could understand why I was not accorded the same respect and dignity in Mississippi as I was in South Dakota and there was nothing I could do about it. I remember the profound sense of not being in control of my self-image as well as the image some Mississipians had of me.

Everything for the eleven months of this stay seemed to speak volumes about what life was all about. I remember going to a movie with a senior law student, from Laurel, Mississippi, and seeing the movie, in black and white, *To kill a mockingbird.*[5] The black people sat in the balcony and I never saw one of them either enter or leave the theater. On the way back to married student housing, on campus, my soon-to-be lawyer companion broke the silence in the car by saying, "That is really scary, this could happen in Mississippi today!" In the fall of 1963, after leaving campus via South Dakota for Wyoming, I was dismayed at the continuation of violence, resulting in not only Medgar Evers being killed but others working in the civil rights movement.

It seemed we were hardly back in Wyoming when the civil rights march in Selma, Alabama, resulted in a son of a family of our church congregation being killed by a blow to the head with a pick handle. A solemn march from the Natrona County Court House to the Natrona County High School gymnasium was made with Roy Wilkins of the NAACP. We listened to words of reassurance from Mr. Wilkins at the gathering in the gymnasium. The loss of Rev. Reeb's life was a jolt to the thought of being secure anywhere in America, for me.

A favorite quote of mine, attributed to Mark Twain, "Never let school interfere with your education," became a true statement of wisdom. I managed to complete the requirements for a Master's degree, but I was set on a course of trying to settle all of the cognitive dissonance this experience created. The cultural shock, of living in Mississippi, was a gift to me that has undoubtedly changed me in ways I would probably never have been moved to do without it. Our family rode the train home at Christmas time and I went to the gumbo farm where I had been reared and went out into a field and stood looking at the prominent land form I had always taken for granted, Bear Butte, a laccolith which stands a few miles north east of the Black Hills. I remember working my feet down into that grayish black gumbo soil and gazing at the Butte for a long time. I finally felt "grounded" enough to go back to Mississippi and finish the degree. I am still working on my education since the school work ended long ago.

It is with this background that I suggest a theory of integrity, knowing that some will ignore it, others may scoff at it, and still others will attack it. However, I am confident a few will listen and maybe alter their own beliefs. My experiences in sharing this theory of integrity with both undergraduate and graduate students over the past fifteen years has been very encouraging. Most of them are open to changing what goes on in their lives - both privately and as professional educators. Many have encouraged me to write this book.

Any theory is everything the word implies. A theory is an idea, a belief or paradigm based upon some verifiable data. A theory is not a fact, it is based upon data which has been found and supports the belief. A theory is constantly being tested for accuracy. When no deviations from the suggested theory are produced the theory remains a theory, possibly a little stronger. When some key aspect of the theory is found to be in discordance or cannot be substantiated, the theory must be re-examined and altered or discarded. Theories are the process by which information and truth is advanced.

This is a technique created to provide a basis for a rational set of actions in the absence of solid facts. This important step goes beyond the reliance upon dogma or doctrine which historically could not be challenged and in Galileo's case, not only resulted in his being silenced but ended scientific discovery in Southern Europe.

As presented in Chapter 6, this theory of integrity is based upon the insights of Hutchins[6] and the field of Holistic[7] medicine. It is difficult for me to believe there are other sources of human energy other than intellectual, emotional, moral, physical and spiritual. My examination of the literature has revealed no others and I have eliminated social as it is sometimes included. This is done because social is an aspect of how one uses the power they have developed.

The geometrical shape of the tetrahedron gives a visual dimension to the theory of integrity, while combining the sources of energy mentioned by Hutchins and the practitioners of holistic medicine. I believe this visual model is a direct reflection of my background in biology and chemistry. Carbon is the element which separates all life forms from the non-living. The carbon atom not only is the basic building block of all life, but is unique in that it conforms to the four peripheral energy centers; intellectual, emotional, moral and physical, but provides a haven or a base of operation for the greater energy source, the spiritual.

Figure 8.1

THEORETICAL MODEL OF INTEGRITY

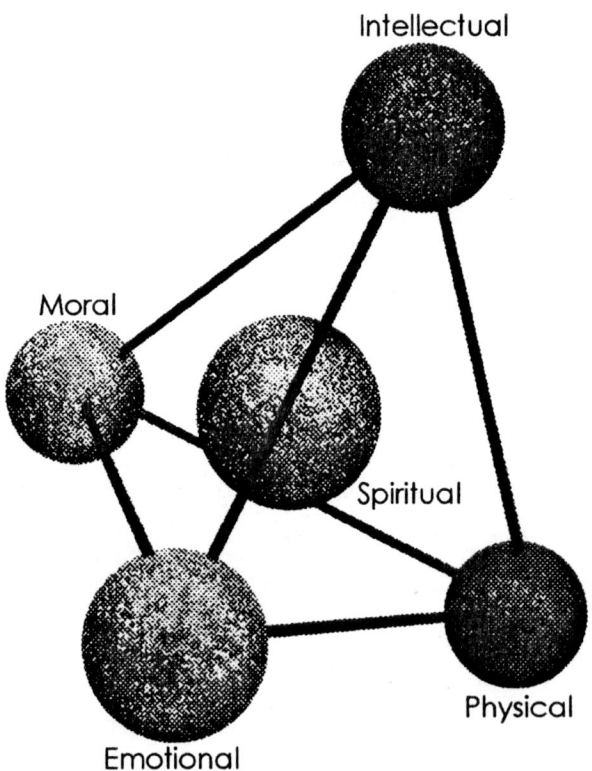

The four corner points (spheres) are the points where the six lines or edges of the tetrahedron connect as shown in Figure 8.1. This visually suggests all energies are connected. Since these four corners are equivalent to the four electrons in a carbon atom's outer energy level, it also suggests that they could not exist in this configuration if it was not for the attraction of a central source of energy, in the case of integrity, this is spiritual. I doubt a person can have much integrity without all five centers, or domains of energy, and reasonably well developed. Without the spiritual source of energy, the person is a hollow shell and will disintegrate and cave in to demands, other than what is good for any human, including himself or herself. A person without spiritual energy or any one of the four corners becomes a two dimensional person.

I believe I went to Mississippi as a two dimensional person, with strength in the areas of moral, physical and intellectual, and very weak in the emotional and spiritual. I believe this is the reason I felt so out of control, like a leaf in those strong winds of change of that time.

My understanding of the atrocities of the Third Reich during World War II are understandable, when using this model, but certainly not defensible. The German people who carried out the inhuman treatment of other humans were one dimensional. They were physically and intellectually strong yet had no core of spiritual strength, let alone any emotional or moral strength. They were apparently completely without compassion or love, feelings or a sense of right and wrong.

I really never read very much until after I went to Mississippi. One didn't need to read anything to get through high school or undergraduate school, so it seemed to me. Now I find that a recent poll of high school students confirmed my suspicions of high school so I can talk about it openly. Since the days of the Mississippi induced cognitive dissonance, I have read more books than I can remember; reading books at every chance I get. The books I have been reading are about emotional or feeling energy and spiritual energy. Most of them, the critical ones, are mentioned throughout this book.

One of the books I frequently refer to, and check my notes in the margins, is R. Buckminster Fuller's book *The critical path.*[8] In Fuller's speculations about the prehistory of humans, human development would not have been possible without the development, in nature, of the tetrahedron. The tetrahedron is a culmination of a sequence, including trajectories, crossings, and openings. He identifies the tetrahedron as the "minimum system of structure."[9]

Those familiar with Fuller's influence, know that he conceived the idea of the "geodesic dome" type of construction using the triangle, one side of a tetrahedron. The tetrahedron is the strongest natural structural combination of matter and energy. Carbon, as a tetrahedron, in the form of an individual atom and loosely associated with the other carbon atoms, is a black powdery substance, soot in a chimney, for example. Yet each carbon atom is a unit of strength in this unconsolidated form. When a multitude of carbon atoms is put under heat and pressure, the individual carbon atoms can be forced into what appears to be a single unit called a diamond. The individual atoms of carbon, because of their individual strengths, when combined in harmony with others, becomes the hardest or strongest naturally occurring substance on earth. A person of high integrity is often called a "gem" of a person.

I am always intrigued, pleased, and encouraged by the reactions of the people to whom this model is presented. Many people make intuitive connections and jumps in awareness, and suggest the soot to diamond analogy. These intuitive insights suggest, to me, they are connecting with something in the theory and something in themselves. It has always motivated me to continue to display and explain the theory as I am doing in this book.

Chapter Nine

The Open System

Many have discussed the equivalent of the open system and some writings contain direct comments about open systems. Robert Samples, *Mind of our mother: toward holonomy and planetary consciousness,* discusses the open mind and then concludes that the mind is an open system.[1] Yet the Western cultures have essentially regarded the mind as a closed system. It is this mistaken notion which I believe has given rise to the maintenance of the closed system culture. One of the major contributors to this closing of the mind was Descartes' assertion that the emotions and feelings were irrational and therefore should be ignored and excluded.[2] It is this control of what is allowed to enter which closes the mind and the culture.

Viktor Frankl in *Man's search for meaning*[3] makes the point that regardless of the degradation and punishment you may endure, you and only you have control over your mind. His survival of the German concentration camp of World War II, called Auschwitz, probably can be attributed to his enduring insight. Although he was a prisoner in camps designed to exterminate people, he survived, probably, because he was able to maintain his mind as an open system. The use of prejudice within the closed system ultimately leads to death as discussed in chapter 4. The closed system function is to take from others and maximize for others. The taking of life is the ultimate end of the closed system. Frankl's open mind about his circumstances provided him a degree of courage, which was unique. Many of those held captive simply gave up and died without being gassed.

Openness is that state of freedom, to access any and all information and freely engage in information processing. The open system encourages the dismantling of culturally held beliefs and traditions. Beliefs and traditions are not considered sacred, only people are sacred. The open system culture always benefits when all beliefs and traditions are examined and constantly reexamined by each succeeding generation. Ideas and information which are passed to succeeding generations through the processes of indoctrination and memorization are not long remembered.

A return to the list of negative cultural practices, specifically those presented in Chapter 3, Figure 3.1, establishes a point from which the positive cultural practices of the open system can be clarified. For every negative factor below the line there is a positive factor that can be chosen instead. For example a culture can practice win/win relationships. Every time a person helps another win, the helper wins and so does the culture. The major commodity in society is knowledge and there is plenty of knowledge for everyone. As a matter of fact knowledge does not exist in a book or on a computer disk, it is only when it has been internalized by a person that it becomes knowledge and therefore useful. Hazel Henderson in *Building a win/win society*, makes a case for information/knowledge being the primary substance of acquisition. With knowledge it is much easier to acquire material wealth.[4] The possession of material wealth does not always guarantee acquisition of knowledge.

Figure 9.1 displays those positive aspects which ultimately produce the open system. The eight items displayed correspond with the eight negative items in Figure 3.1. The placement of the positive above the shaft of the arrow and the negative below the arrow was determined only because of the long standing precedent of heaven and hell. There is no other connection or inference intended in this arrangement.

The positive aspect, listed first, optimism, is a positive attitudinal condition; a learned choice. Seligman has developed an educational approach to teaching optimism. He defines optimism as believing:

> . . .defeat is just a temporary setback, that its causes are confined to this one case. The optimists believe defeat is not their fault: Circumstances, bad luck, or other people brought it about. Such people are unfazed by defeat. Confronted by a bad situation, they perceive it as a challenge and try harder.[5]

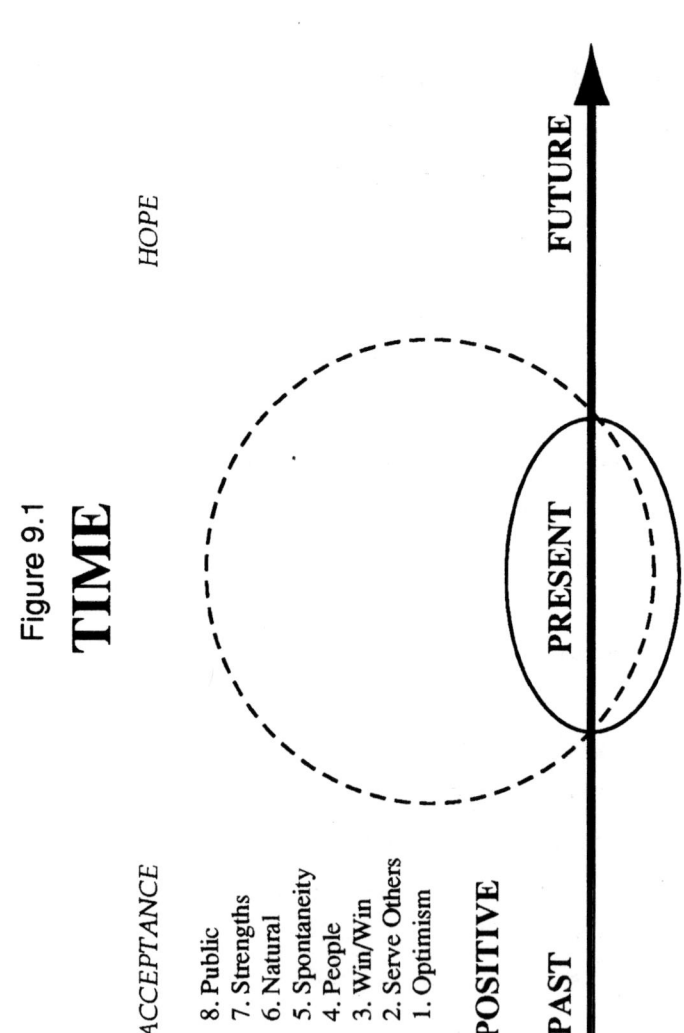

Figure 9.1

People who are optimistic tend to be healthier, thus escaping many of the ills of middle age, and therefore live longer.[6]

My own data, collected over 14 years, shows that positive people make better teachers and often become more positive as they continue in teaching. People who self select to become junior and senior high teachers are more negative than those who choose to become elementary teachers. A major effort, of mine, was to increase the positiveness of those choosing to be secondary teachers. Much of the material presented in this book became part of the teacher education program. Over the 14 years there was no statistical difference in any of the 28 groups of teacher education majors on their positiveness of attitude scores at the outset of the professional semester. However, as time passed and as new dimensions were added to the educational program, two important trends developed. The first trend was a very significant increase in the positiveness of attitude before doing student teaching. The second trend was a significant holding of the positiveness of attitude after the student teaching experience.[7] This suggests to me there are probably a number of ways to teach optimism or positiveness of attitude.

The second entry in Figure 9.1 is a predisposition to serve others instead of control them. Servant leadership, as described by Greenleaf[8], is seeing someone in need and applying one's efforts to helping achieve the success they desire. This type of relationship produces highly capable people in the cases of both those being served and the one doing the serving. This is a natural relationship, since all people come into the world limited in their abilities. The only way someone learns is through the efforts of someone who already knows and then is willing to help them learn it too. The negative aspect of controlling people leads only to incompetence on the parts of those needing to learn and those who could serve them.

Looking at the world as an arena in which everyone wins makes winners out of everyone. This win/win approach makes more time available for the servant to help the more needy and some of the recent benefactors of learning can also help with the truly needy. The end result or goal is that all shall share in the advantages of the cultural benefits which have accrued. I am sure if this approach was taken, there would be a significant drop in the need for prisons and a dramatic need for an increase in colleges or other educational establishments. Effective coaches practice many of the win/win principles in that they do not grade the athletes on a bell curve. The coach has as the main goal of the coaching, that everyone on the team will master the skills needed for this activity. Win/win principles are alive and active in society to a limited extent.

It is obvious the focus of the win/win approach is upon people instead of material things. A person who is struggling to accomplish some task, who is helped to learn that task, is immediately a new resource in the culture. This is in contrast to the win/lose approach which sees people as obstacles to success and therefore sees them as things to be manipulated and even discarded. When each person is recognized as a gift to the world, it is much easier to be of service to him or her rather than to try to control them. Children who are treated as gifts to the world are full of adventure and creative energy. This creative energy is encouraged and welcomed, because it means new possibilities for the benefit of the individual and the culture.

The fifth entry on the list of positives is spontaneity. People whose sacredness, as a gift, is welcomed and honored are free to take many risks in a world full of unlimited possibility. This spontaneity gives a newness and freshness of life to whatever they do. Often these spontaneous individuals appear child like in their curiosity and inventiveness. I am reminded of a fifteen year old youth who had decided to acquire a complete set of keys to the junior high school. David was not a bad boy in any sense of the word. He devised the most ingenious method of getting keys by utilizing his personal traits of honesty and trustworthiness. David told only one lie to gain control of one master key and from there he would enter the building on weekends and holidays to search classrooms and offices for additional keys. His goal was to have a complete set of keys. A conference with his parents soon helped him see that his creativity would be better spent preparing for college. Much of what is pure unadulterated spontaneity is never recognized but discouraged and punished when it is revealed. This is a tremendous loss to the individual and the culture. The adrenaline released by those who are inquisitive, inventive, and spontaneous is the natural substitute for addiction from the effects of living in a negatively driven culture. There simply is no need to sedate pain artificially when living spontaneously in the present moment. The soul constantly encourages the expression of spontaneous creativity.

All things of creation, which includes humans, are part of the natural world. The dualism of tame/wild has no place in the positive world above the line. There is no need to defeat anything or destroy anything since all living things share the same elements from the environment. When humans are seen as a natural part of the entire creation, then attempts at maintaining harmony among all segments, both physical and biological, are the issues of main concern. Differences are seen at worst as only differences, but at the best, all differences are seen as new possibilities and therefore as strengths. A person who can look at another person who is quite different and see them as a valuable resource to others brings awareness to everyone and strength to the group.

When the revolution occurred in Hungary in the late 1950's and many fled to the United States, a family came to the community where I was just beginning my career as a teacher. One of the boys was a student in one of my classes. When school resumed on a Monday, I asked what anyone had done that was exciting over the weekend. A student mentioned he had gone to Billings, Montana from his home in Casper, Wyoming. John, the boy from Hungary, said with utter astonishment, "How did you do that?" A chorus of students said, "It is easy, just get in the car and drive to Billings." John said, "I can't believe it, in Hungary you would have to have a visa, if you could get one." Everyone learned about how different things are in different countries.

Item seven in the list identifies relating to strengths in others. In John's case, a family fleeing for their lives and freedom, helped the other students understand a serious condition in another part of the world and they helped John understand what his new found freedom could mean. No one was looked upon as being weak or stupid. Everyone was ignorant of something but everyone was knowledgeable about something that others could benefit from knowing. My experiences provide many memories which are examples of people with uniqueness, that is all too often labeled as a weakness. I went to under graduate school with a fellow who did not have a left arm yet he could swim and play basketball better than 90 percent of the people in school. How could he swim and play better than people with no limbs missing? What some saw as a defect or weakness in him was not that at all in the activities of swimming and basketball. Most of all he was probably less self-conscious in the presence of others than most.

A person who is self-confident has no need to try to keep secrets and puts all of his or her energy into being who they are. People who live above the line, and in the open system, are aware that some things are private but they have not secrets. The energy saved by not concealing secrets makes it possible for them to be more alive in the present moment and less likely to become protective of the private matters in their lives. I am reminded of President Eisenhauer's lying about the U-2 spy plane shot down over Russia. When he admitted the United States had been routinely flying spy missions over Russia, his popularity as a President improved. Often junior high students would ask questions about how to know what they should do in given situations. I would just as routinely ask them if they would like to explain what they were doing to their parents. I would tell them if the answer was no, then don't do it.

People who choose to live above the line find life much more fulfilling and joyous because they feel alive in the present moment. They have a deeper appreciation of the past and can look to the future with greater and more positive anticipation. When people are related to, through optimism, service, win/win, as a gift, spontaneity, as a part of nature, strengths and publicly validated and accepted in the fullest way possible, they are much more capable. These people see hope and love as constant conditions which feed the desire to explore the fullest dimensions of being human. The people with more complete memories of the past, have the greatest sense of the present moment because of the safe structure in society created through acceptance. Living above the line is a choice made by the individual based upon the experiences of life. Children who experience the power of adults who are alive in the present moment are freer, more creative, and experience more enjoyment from life in general.

The preceding has been an example of how it is possible to build or put together something positive by contrasting it with the disassembled negative dimensions of the closed system. Taking an idea or concept apart and understanding it from the cultural perspective of those who created it renders it a useful part of a person's memory, never to be completely forgotten. An example is the lesson which is taught in schools repeatedly, because so few remember it, is that of location on the earth by measures of latitude and longitude. As soon as people understand the origin of this concept comes from the people who navigated the Mediterranean Sea, it becomes embedded in the memory. The key words used today, were chosen at the time this important understanding was developed, because longitude means long or length, and latitude means width or to the side. Therefore movements on the earth east and west, the long way of the Mediterranean Sea and movements to the north and south, the width of the Sea it all makes sense, although the earth itself is a sphere. A second advantage for the culture comes from the possibilities of correcting some errors in the original idea or concept as well as a much greater possibility of a creative breakthrough of a whole new idea.

Another example of learning what the ancients so diligently worked out and have left as a legacy, is the concept of the Greek letter π used in calculations involving circles. Most generally, students are taught to memorize that π has a numerical value of 3.1416 and its numerical value is to be inserted into the formula in place of the symbol for purposes of calculation. A simple exercise which clarifies this important constant, is to have a class working in groups of two or three, measure the diameter of a roll of tape and the length of the outer layer of tape, which they remove and lay flat on the desk top. They all get different measurements because they all have different sizes of rolls of tape, but they all get the same answer when then divide the circumference by the diameter. It is then that the constant, the ancients named pi (π), becomes a meaningful part of the students' memories.

The open system is a win-win system and is therefore of benefit to all people. The closed system, as a win-lose system, is an attempt to create advantages for those in authority at the expense of those not holding power. In fact there is no such thing as a win-lose system on the long range scheme of things. A person who gains a short term advantage at the expense of another, is always bound to that person. This became abundantly clear to me when I lived in Mississippi. The white culture could never seem to get more than an arms length away from the black people they were exploiting. If the black people were not there to be exploited it seemed to me, the white people would have had even less.

The open system is all of the area outside of the encircled section on the sigmoid curve in Figure 9.2. The existence of humans was probably an open system before the time of 10,000 years ago when all people were probably living the nomadic way of life. Evidence indicates the beginnings of agriculture were the beginning of the closed (mind) system. You may benefit from reviewing Figure 4.2 in chapter four.

The open system is in fact the age of compassion, as described by Marilyn Ferguson in *The Aquarian conspiracy*.[9] The old ways, of either going to war or playing games, are of the closed system and therefore always work to the disadvantage of someone or some group known as the losers in the closed system. The open system relies upon love, encouragement, and discipline. You will recall the closed system is driven by prejudice, praise, and punishment. The closed system drains off the energy of people into defending and getting

116   Alvin W. Holst

Figure 9.2
POPULATION GROWTH CURVE
(Sigmoid Curve)

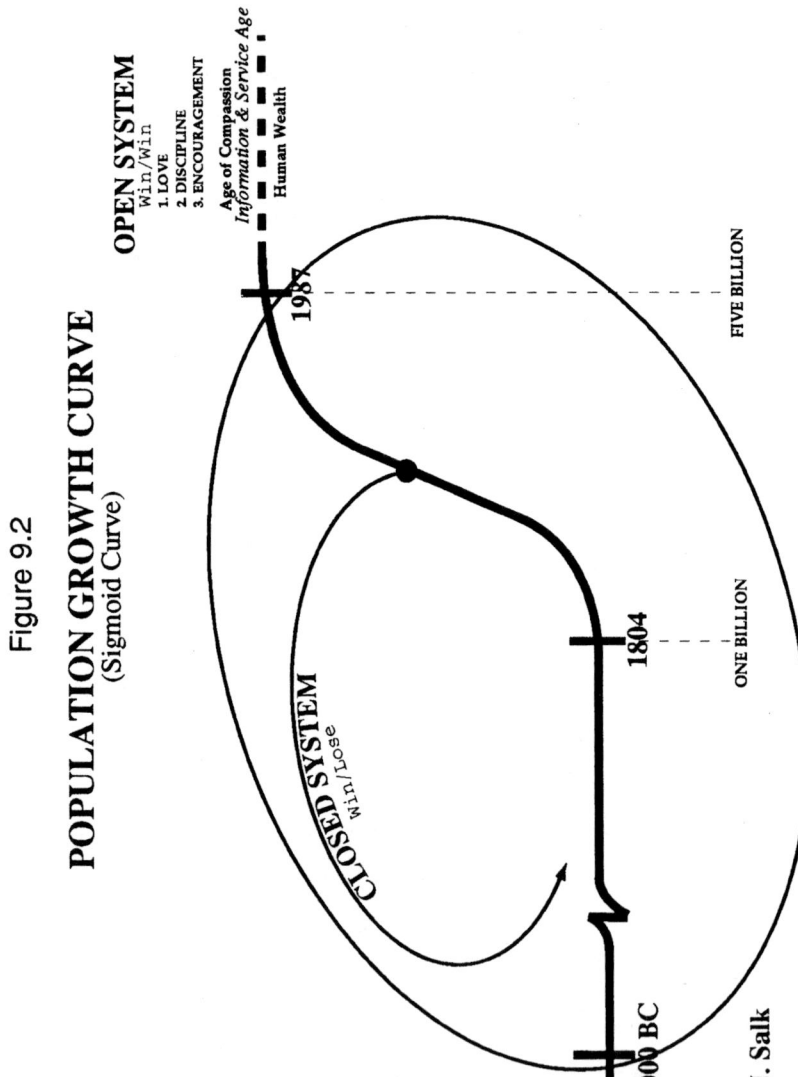

even or worse, becoming depressed and giving up. The open system liberates the individual so this energy is available to promote growth in others.

Love is spiritual energy, which all human beings can develop. People in the closed system identify love as an important commodity and try to get all they can while not giving any away. Love is not nurtured by hoarding it as though there is a scarcity. Remember the concept of scarcity is a negative element which helps drive the closed system. Loving skills are learned early in life, but can be developed at any age.

Love is the willingness to believe those things which are true and positive. (Remember prejudice is the willingness to believe those things which are false and negative.) This definition of love is the flip or positive side of Allport's[10] conception of prejudice. Therefore the first step is **believing** - those things which are true and positive. This is completely under the control of the individual, although the closed system encourages prejudice, it does not have to be chosen.

Most people ask for assistance in changing beliefs to be positive. My standard response is to name two fundamental beliefs, which have dramatically changed my life and how I relate to myself and others. The first belief is, *"Any given person, at a any given moment, is doing the very best he or she can."* Initially, this belief is often difficult for many to accept. There are generally many arguments offered to refute such a positive and truthful statement. The problem seems to be associated with the concept of time, and people are sure the person *could* do better. It is true that the person could do better, but at that moment he or she is doing the best he or she can. The example of the person who has over indulged in alcohol and at the moment is face down in a gutter, lying in his or her own vomit, is doing the very best possible at that moment. Yes, they could have done better in the past, but now this the best.   Those people who are emotionally out of control and yelling and ranting are doing the best they can, at that moment. The only alternative you have is to *accept* them and what they are doing as their best, at that moment. It is only then that you can act out of love and offer hope to them. The closed system encourages disdain and disgust for failures, which are acts of rejection and dehumanization of a gift to the world.

It is, I have found, easier for people to accept the first statement when the second statement is revealed. *"Regardless of how poorly or well a person is doing, he or she wants to do better."* Olympic athletes who win gold medals all want to do even better. I am sure the youthful Tiger Woods wants to be an even better golfer, in spite of his record breaking win of the 1997 Masters. Even the drunkard wants to do better or the abusive person wants to do better. Whether these statements are in fact true, is less important than whether a person can internalize them and consistently act upon them. To the extent a person chooses to relate to others as, *"this is your best and I know you want to do better,"* these beliefs become more positive and true. We, in fact create exactly what we believe, negative or positive. What is happening in the world today is the collective effect of the prevailing beliefs of people, nothing more, nothing less. If a person wants less negativity in the world, he or she should choose to be more positive.

Once we adopt positive and more truthful beliefs, then we should spend our time **talking** about them. In fact that is what this whole book is about. Often, aspiring teachers have asked, "What does someone mean when they say, 'If you want to be happy as a teacher, stay out of the teachers lounge?'" They soon find out during the student teaching experience. They are appalled at the amount of prejudice which is expressed by closed system teachers.

The next step of acting out of love, instead of going to the lounge to gossip in prejudicial terms, is effort at **seeking** or finding those who are in greatest need. The true champions, as teachers, are those who willingly seek out the needy student and serve them with kindness, acceptance, and understanding. The closed system teacher avoids these kids and is therefore of no value to anyone. Even the capable students are fearful of needing help for fear of only being denied help, when they really need it.

As the chairperson for a junior high science department, I was given a class period to manage the affairs and equipment of the department. I was able to enlist the aide of a student to work one period a day in the science storeroom and keep things cleaned, put away, and inventoried. One young lad, I found, who I knew very well in school, had a problematic life outside of school. Once, he had burglarized a house during the day time, for example. I offered him the job of being the student aide in the science storeroom during his ninth grade year. About three weeks after school started the next fall, one of the teaching staff came to me in a state or real disgust and said, "Do you know anything about who you have working in the science storeroom." And I told him I knew as much about him as anyone and he needed to have something important to do. The teacher said, "Then don't expect me to use any of the science equipment or supplies as long as I have to go through him." It was amazing to me, that a teacher would deprive all of the students in his classes, because he didn't like one student in the school. Incidentally, Wes was the best student aide we ever had, we never lost a single thing, not even a broken test tube. By involving him in a meaningful way, his life became more meaningful and important to him.

The next step of love is to involve people by **including** them in special ways. Special ways means to recognize and honor their strengths, which everyone has, in ways that are meaningful to them and everyone else. As people work from their strengths they are better able to work on those areas in need of development. Where prejudice encourages exclusion, love is inclusion. Love is very possible, because people do in fact belong, because they are the ultimate gifts to the world.

The fifth step of love, still paralleling Allport's[11] steps of prejudice, is **stroking**. Stroking is a concept taken from Transactional Analysis (TA) and accurately describes the appropriate response. Where the prejudice provides verbal and physical assault, love makes contact verbally by *encouragement* rather than praise and physically by touching the person. I have seen elementary students come to school very ill with the flu, just so they could get a "high-five" from the Physical Education teacher. A pat on the back or a good shoulder to shoulder hug are helpful to someone struggling, who needs to make contact with the real world and know everything is okay. Thomas Harris in *I'm OK - you're OK: a practical guide to transactional analysis* points to the tender stroking a person receives at the time of birth as extremely important to psychological birth. "This is the first incoming data that life "out there" isn't all bad."[12] This physical contact of caring, concern and acceptance is communicated as empathy and support. The closed system offers sympathy, which most people find empty and degrading. All violations of another's integrity take place in the closed system and therefore, what is often passed off as stroking in the closed system is really and attempt at exploitation. One of the more difficult tasks of being a school principal, for me, was the responsibility to stop the sexual caressing of students by teachers, and thus end the person's career as a teacher. The open system requires everyone, not just children, youth, and females, to be vulnerable. Open system people see this as a sacred trust and the closed system people see it as license to do as they please.

The sixth and last step of love involves the actual creation of a new human and promoting growth in them. Therefore **birthing** and **growing** are the sacred purposes of human life instead of killing to which prejudice ultimately leads. As parents, it is important that the creation of the child came from the first five steps of love instead of from lust and/or rape. I would like to believe that all humans are then the epitome of two people acting totally out of love. The number of unwanted pregnancies suggest otherwise. I believe the unwanted pregnancies are a symptom of the closed system. I honestly believe, if a person is strong in integrity he or she would not act out of the sheer joy of the moment. I am sure that many who become sexually active before they are intellectually, emotionally, morally, and spiritually responsible, do so as another form of addiction. Sex is used as a form of escape or diversion from the pain of the soul they are experiencing due to a lack of proper development of the energies which promote integrity.

The second trait of an open system is discipline. Discipline in the open system replaces punishment in the closed system. The misuse of the word discipline is confusing as was discussed in chapter 4. What is done in the name of discipline is almost totally punishment. Discipline comes from a root word which means teaching and learning, which is the preferred definition in the dictionary. Punishment only teaches how to make someone hurt or be forcibly obedient. Discipline happens when people take the time to find the cause behind the inappropriate behavior and then teach the skills which make it possible for the person to function much more capably.

The first year as principal in a junior high, I noted the large amount of fighting which was going one among the students and began to look for causes. After many consultations with the teaching staff, inability of the students to read very well, seemed to be a recurring issue. It was decided to test all the students in the school for reading ability. The finding was shocking, one out of every three seventh graders was at least two years or more below grade level. The eighth and ninth grade had a ratio of about one out of every four students at least two or more years below grade level. When the second semester began, every seventh grade student and most of the eighth and ninth grade students were taken out of an elective and put into developmental reading classes. The student fighting was significantly reduced, not because everyone suddenly learned to read, but rather because they were learning how to read better. Punishment was definitely not the appropriate response to the fighting, but rather the discipline of learning how to read better was. I know of a high school graduate who said, "It is (expletive deleted) pathetic that I never learned to read in school." This statement was accompanied by an outpouring of anger and tears.

The third trait of the open system is the use of encouragement instead of praise. The most complete source of information about encouragement is Don Dinkmeyer and Lewis Losoncy's book, *The encouragement book: becoming a positive person.*[13] Encouragement focuses upon a person's ability to manage themselves from an internal orientation through feedback on "effort and improvement."[14] The assets of the person or his or her strengths become the focal point of the encouraging, so the person learns self-evaluation. Encouragement establishes acceptance and therefore openness. The person's worth is never in question as it is with praise.

Not only is this paradigm the Age of Compassion, but it is also the *Information and Service Age.* The successes of the two previous paradigms, the Age of War and the Age of Games have been very effective in moving humanity toward a time when enough food and material/energy wealth is available to sustain the population. With humans at this juncture in cultural evolution the big question is, "What are we going to do with this wealth?" The closed system interests are continually suggesting preparing for war, play more games and by all means keep the majority of people deprived of the wealth, lest they not be willing to clean our toilets and empty our garbage.

The open system has an entirely different agenda. The focus or thrust of the open system approach, is the application of the wealth toward the development of every citizen as a free participant in the most highly evolved democracy in the history of the world. This translates into the creation of *human wealth*. There is more than enough information to help every person become a more fully functioning citizen. The challenge ahead for the American culture is whether there is enough courage and soul to use the massive accumulations of material wealth for human development or human destruction. It is an awesome moral opportunity that faces the American culture. Humanity is poised in a manner never before so profoundly obvious to so many.

PART THREE

ACHIEVING INTEGRITY

"When the stomach speaks wisdom is silent." (Arab Proverb)

"A peaceful person is the first criterion if you want to have a peaceful universe. You start with the universe you've got, which is your own being." (Baba Ram Das)

"It is the tragedy of the world that no one knows what he doesn't know - and the less a man knows, the more sure he is that he knows everything." (Joyce Cary)

"I realized a long time ago that a belief which does not spring from a conviction in the emotions is no belief at all." (Evelyn Scott)

"The great tragedy of life is not that men perish, but that they cease to love." (W. Somerset Maughm)

"We do not usually look for allies when we love. Indeed, we often look on those who love with us as rivals and trespassers. But we always look for allies when we hate." (Eric Hoffer)

"There is a law that man should love his neighbor as himself. In a few hundred years it should be as natural to mankind as breathing or the upright gait; but if he does not learn it, he must perish." (Alfred Adler)

Part three continues the sequence of questioning started in parts one and two, which addressed the why and what issues of integrity. Part three provides clues to identifying the elements of integrity. When people do not recognize their sources of energy or how well these areas of self are developed, they live as enigmas. They are more a puzzle to themselves than anyone but are not easily understood by others either.

The fullest measure of integrity comes from extensive development in at least the five domains of energy previously discussed. The complete person has strength in intellect, emotion, physical, moral, and spirit. They are said to be alive in the present moment and are not relying upon external sets of rules to guide them in their daily activities.

Integrity as a state of existence gives the person the power to call upon each of the five sources of energy as needed. This is truly an empowered person in the fullest sense of the term. Integrity also means the person knows how to access the energy sources and combine them appropriately to the situation.

It is easier to change if a person has a measure of where they function in relation to where they want to be functioning. Self-evaluation is the key element in human development; for if the person does not know where he or she is functioning in relation to where he or she would like to be functioning, it makes little difference what they do, because they will not arrive at the place they seek. The following five chapters are devoted to each of the five areas of energy and how a person can begin to improve in the areas or domains they choose.

Chapter Ten

Intellectual Power

The intellect is a facet of human existence which has been a deciding factor in the ability of humans to evolve. It provides the great breakthroughs which are required for advancement and hopefully for the improvement of conditions within the culture. Unfortunately history is replete with examples of the deterioration of human conditions. When someone "figures out" something new it is immediately passed on to others. This great new insight then becomes one of the memes[1] of the culture to be passed along in addition with the genes. This blending of gene and meme influence has been the basis of much contemplation about heredity and environment. The lack of a clear resolution, of which of the two is the more influential, is not a concern for the discussion to follow.

Once this new idea, which is represented in subsequent behavior, "escapes" into the world it is like the genie that escapes from the bottle. There is evidence this psychic energy floats in space within the culture as indicated by Morris Berman in *Coming to our senses: body and spirit in the hidden history of the west.*[2] The person with whom the new idea originated may die of natural causes, or in the closed system, be put to death, but the idea takes on a life of its own. Since the closed system is all about control of others then these ideas are treated as disease germs when they contradict the prevailing social practices. They must be exterminated. The message of love, that Jesus Christ brought to the world, was an unwelcome message, so the messenger was killed on bogus charges.

In other cases these new ideas have been accepted by those in authority and deliberate attempts have been made to transmit them to succeeding generations with considerable success. Gutenberg's printing press, of the fifteenth century, changed the course of history. This new advantage also made is harder for those in authority to control the thinking processes of those chosen for exploitation. The issue of censorship has forever been a concern. People who read can ultimately think about things differently than they are commanded to think. This always leads to some kind of insurrection which leads to banning the objectionable reading materials and the authors. Intellectual development has always been the curse or demon for closed system practices. Since censorship is a form of oppression, it not only weakens the intellect of the oppressed but it also weakens the intellect of the oppressors. Intellectual development is halted when censorship is invoked.

The argument that some things are "unthinkable" is a justification for trying to keep people from thinking about those things the authorities do not want them to think about. It has long been known that when people think about things, their subsequent behaviors are affected. Therefore to keep people compliant and unchallenging of authority they must have their thinking closely controlled. Charges of heresy, blasphemy, treason, and being un-patriotic are all used in a closed system to justify preventing any movement away from the practices of the authorities within the culture. The practice of censorship is akin to robbing people of the freedom of their mind and therefore enslaves them to the culturally intended ignorance. "What people don't know won't hurt them. It is for their own good that they remain ignorant." The paternalistic ways of the closed system, makes dependent victims out of those it is ostensibly taking care of for their own good.

The identification of the cultural attempts at controlling the intellect is the major thrust of this chapter. When the intellect is developed in every citizen, ignorance does not hold them hostage or limit their freedom. When people are being physically held in bondage, they can extricate themselves by using the power of the intellect. This was never more clear to me than when I lived in Mississippi. It was so obvious that blacks had been systematically denied the intellectual development every human needs to the point they had taken over the responsibly of their own continued oppression. The blacks did not know what they did not know, the same as anyone living in ignorance. The difference was, they knew less of everything than the whites. In those days, in Mississippi, is was the practice to set off fireworks at Christmas time rather than on the Fourth of July. The explanation was that it would cause too many questions about life, liberty and the pursuit of happiness. "Better to keep them ignorant of the U.S. Constitution and how it applies to all humans." Ignorance is the tool of the closed system.

The intellect is more than it has come to be thought of in the Western world. Western thought has settled almost exclusively upon capabilities of the left hemisphere of the brain. The linear thought, talking, seeing the pieces, absence of emotion, rational, analytic, sequential, and preference for hierarchy are left hemisphere characteristics. This is a product of the Western thought with its roots deep in the ancient Greek culture.

The Old Testament of the Bible was written in Hebrew from the right hemisphere (the right hemisphere will be discussed subsequently). The New Testament was written in Greek from the left hemisphere. The left brain explanations of the O T are no more plausible than the right brain explanations of N T. The Bible suggests that our ancestors were primarily right brained until the time of the Greek Empire when the left brain began to be accessed and developed. This practice was not totally acceptable in ancient Athens as Socrates was charged with corrupting the youth and sentenced to death by drinking the juice of Hemlock. His method, known today as Socratic questioning, fortunately survived his death and was passed along by his star pupil, Plato.

Native American or Indian students are largely right brained as determined by giving them the *Hemispheric Mode Indicator (HMI)* developed and marketed by Excel, Inc.[3] A graduate student, who taught biology in a parochial school on the Pine Ridge Reservation, gave this instrument to the students of his Biology classes and found that the only students doing well had developed left brain characteristics. Unfortunately this was fewer than ten percent of the students.

The Western culture has promoted an educational system that does not honor the total make-up of the person. Left hemisphere learning has been pushed as the center piece of the curricula to the exclusion of right hemisphere curricula. Case in point; the elimination or drastic curtailment of the fine arts curricula always occurs during tight economic times. The schools which serve the students from backgrounds of deprivation, also lack right brain educational practices for students who may already be lacking in left brain characteristics.

Another graduate student told me after seeing the results of his own HMI score that he was dramatically relieved. In his nearly forty years of life he had basically concluded he was mentally defective because of his educational experiences. His response was, "Now I know what has been wrong, it is not me. I have been unsuccessful in school because I am a right brain student in left brain schools." I suspect that much of the labeling that goes on in schools could be done away with if more attention was given to hemisphere concerns in curriculum development and teaching practices. As a matter of record, Madeline Hunter[4] developed a system of teaching which includes both right and left brain practices.

Right brain learning is probably the first kind of learning that anyone does, to be followed later by left brain learning, but preferably not at the expense of continued right brain learning. I see a potential problem in educational practices which are designed to develop the left hemisphere, being offered much before the age of six years. Plato did not recommend formal education begin before age six. His reasons may not have been based upon the reductionist type of educational research of today but rather upon his right brain intuitive sense. Some kindergarten and early childhood schools start pushing the left brain curriculum and probably cause learning difficulties for the child. A child who cannot learn the left brain curriculum experiences school in a way that makes him or her begin to develop a sense of being a failure. This is not the intended outcome of this pre-school experience, so when it happens, "it must be some defect in the child," according to the proponents of left brain learning in pre-school. Another case of blaming the victim.

The right brain is intuitive. Culturally we have seen intuitiveness denigrated and I suspect that is because it is seen as feminine. "Woman's intuition" has never been as highly regarded as the male "gut feeling." Although men are completely capable of right brain intuition they would never want to be thought of as effeminate. The right brain is open-ended, looks for patterns, is fluid, relies on images in thinking and remembering, expresses emotions, sees the whole and is mute. Some artists are unable to speak or describe what they are doing while in the act of doing it. Mel Tillis, as a singer, is a good example of left brain - right brain characteristics. His stuttering when he speaks is explained by an inability to freely move to the left hemisphere while his singing ability from his right hemisphere has made him famous.

Much is yet to be learned about how the brain works. A good deal of what is now known, however, is not respected in the educational setting. At this point it is sufficient to say that when the curriculum and the teaching practices are adapted and consistently presented to both hemispheric orientations to learning, greater intellectual development occurs. The twenty-first century will be a time of great break-throughs in learning, that will be more liberating and less enslaving. The open system will be in full bloom when all children master the formal and intended curricula.

Another aspect of the intellect is contained in the orientation to how people approach learning or their style. This was first suggested by Carl Jung[5] and has seen great adaptation in the decades of eighties and nineties. Although there are several adaptations of Jung's idea, the one I have chosen to present here has been the distillation of many by Bernice McCarthy of Excel, Inc.[6] Style theory suggests there are four approaches or styles to learning which accompany brain orientation. These can be called either learning styles or leadership styles because they are orientations to problem solving.

McCarthy has numbered them 1 through 4 for the purposes of identifying where effective teaching begins and ends.[7] Effective teaching begins with style 1 and both hemispheres of the brain, the question is *why* this lesson. Style 1 learners are interested in the relevance of the lesson and if everyone will enjoy the experience. Style 2 answers the question *what* is this lesson about, which is what has always passed as traditional teaching. Style 2 learners are interested in the correctness of the lesson and may not begin until this is settled. Many teachers are not comfortable teaching in some of these styles in spite of having students of all four styles in their classes. This situation leads to more exclusion of those who don't learn in the same way the teacher teaches. All teachers are more effective when they teach to all four styles and both brain orientations.

Style 3 is the guided practice part of the teaching and shows *how* what is to be learned, can be learned. Style 3 people are motivated to get things done even if it means not following the rules or directions, although they prefer to follow the rules. Style 4 teaching is directed to applying the newly learned material in creative ways and applying it to the real world. Style 4 people seek excitement and surprise in what they do and are concerned that they are liked by those with whom they associate. Their excitement for new possibilities leads them not to be comfortable within an hierarchical structure.

You will recall this book is laid out in four parts. This is done deliberately to reflect the orientations to learning of the readers. It is suggested in the introduction that the reader may wish to begin reading wherever his or her interest is initially the greatest. However the reader is strongly urged to read the book in its entirety to get the integrated package of information.

In using the *Learning Style Inventory* (LSI)[8] for more than a dozen years, I have found the majority of people, going out to be teachers, are either Style 1 or 4. This seems logical in that these two styles are more interested in relationships than in tasks. As a matter of my experience, as a principal in junior high schools, I found that teachers who were the least concerned with relationships had more student behavior problems.

I have administered the LSI to experienced teachers and find that most of them are Style 1 and 4. The few Style 3 people who go into teaching usually also coach some athletic teams where they can "get things done." Traditionally most of the administrators come from the ranks of style 3 teachers. Another interesting group of people to whom I have administered the LSI was a group of my professorial peers. The majority of these people are Style 2. I am a style 2 person. I once had a class that was over sixty percent Style 2. They were a very intimidating class to teach because of the predisposition to not move unless it was "correct." The other three styles which by nature are usually quite talkative fell silent in this class, more silent than the style 2 students.

Hunter who was mentioned earlier developed the ITIP program which parallels McCarthy's 1 through 4 style approach with hemispheric provisions.[9]

When another set of characteristics of learning is factored in, called modalities, of which there are three, the product is twenty-four possible types of learners in a typical classroom. The four learning styles, two brain orientations and three modalities looks like this mathematically (4 X 2 X 3 = 24). The closed system school typically recognizes only one of these 24 possibilities. Traditional teaching is usually Style 2, Left hemisphere and Auditory (lecturing or talking at the students). This not only presents problems for teachers but especially for students.

Modalities are another facet of learning and are sometimes given other names. The instrument which I have used is called *The Learning Channel Preference Checklist*(LCPC).[10] For our purpose here, I will use the term modality since it reflects the person's preference for the sense most commonly used. Visual, auditory and haptic represent the senses of sight, hearing and touch respectively. People have developed a preference based upon which is reliably the most effective for them. Most people are visually dominant and the least number of people are auditorially inclined. Historically and paradoxically, lecturing has been the predominate mode of transmitting the intellectual part of the curriculum.

My first conscious educational experience with modalities was with a class of eighth grade students in science during the 1966-67 school year. These were the days of large class sizes of 35-40 students. That school year I had a class with two students I had previously never given much thought as to how to teach them. One boy was legally blind, (he had been born prematurely and a twin and therefore placed in an oxygen tent only to have the oxygen destroy the corneas of his eyes) and a girl who was profoundly deaf from an inherited trait. Everything I said, so the blind student could hear, I had to write on the chalk board, so the deaf student could see it. That experience taught me the value of teaching to all modalities, the whole class benefited from this approach. The concept of intelligence has been around a long time but it took on new meaning in the French schools when a Medical Doctor, Alfred Binet, was asked to devise a way to screen out from the regular classes those students, between the ages of three and twelve years, who were intellectually inferior and incapable of normal learning.[11] Dr. Binet's system, has been refined to produce an *intelligence quotient (IQ)*. To determine IQ, divide the child's intellectual age(development) by the child's chronological age and then multiply that value by one hundred. Obviously the child who knows what his age group is expected to know, has an IQ of 100. However if a child of eight years of age knows what a child of ten knows his IQ score could be 120. The child of eight years of age who knows no more than a child of six may have an IQ score of 75. Now this measurement was only a comparison of children of that day in France. However it has been applied in ways that suggest that IQ is inherited and therefore not changeable, as many have asserted.

A raging debate has taken place from time to time over one group within the American society being intellectually superior due to genetic programming. Arthur Jensen while at Berkeley claimed this to be the case for Blacks, Irish, Mexicans, Indians but not for Eskimos.[12] At a presentation of his, in 1971, on Campus at Arizona State University, he was unable to give an explanation to a question from the audience of how he controlled for the effects of oppression upon intellectual development. He apparently did not understand the effects of cultural memes. His following was never strong and eventually he did not report or push his findings. In the decade of the nineties, this notion of intellect following racial and ethnic lines again surfaced in *The bell curve: intelligence and class structure in American life* written by Herrnstein and Murray.[13] A refutation, of this racist position by twenty notable scholars, was published as *The bell curve wars: race, intelligence, and the future of America.*[14]

The concept of intelligence being fixed at birth, was further strengthened by the work of Thorndike. During World War I, the military found that of the more than a million recruits, many were of limited intellectual ability. The American Psychological Association appointed a committee to help in the war effort. Thorndike and others developed a group IQ test to be given at the time of induction. This changed the Binet test from a singly administered test to a group test. The Thorndike version (commonly known as the Lorge-Thorndike) soon found its way into public schools as a way of sorting students for special services.[15] All of this early testing was done upon unfounded assumptions of IQ being set for life at the time of birth and specific to the racial or ethnic group.

A broader and more inclusive approach to a fuller and more accurate understanding has been under way both at Harvard and Yale. I heard Howard Gardner, of Harvard University, speak at the conference in Tarrytown, New York shortly after his book, *Frames of mind*,[16] was first published. His theory of multiple intelligences has found wide acceptance. His belief of seven different intelligences definitely broadens the scope of what intelligence probably is. Only one of these seven intelligences is measured by standard IQ tests or other measures of academic ability such as SATs. His theories are being developed for inclusion in the curricula to teach to all seven intelligences.

It seemed almost simultaneously Robert Sternberg[17] had put forth the theory of three intelligences. Only one of these is equivalent to the standard earlier belief of intelligence. In both cases, Gardner and Sternberg have addressed intelligence from a more open system approach. These efforts are contributing to improvements of not only what intelligence is but what can be done to see that potential is more fully developed.

The Termin studies, done in California, over fifty years ago were an attempt to find out how exceptionally intelligent people contribute later in life to society.[18] The first follow-up study was conducted forty years after the students had been identified. The findings did not reveal any great societal contributions from these people so identified. As a group they were no different from the general population of so called average students. As a matter of fact the greatest contributors are invariably from the average student population. As a school principal, I was uneasy with the thrust to identify and place students in gifted programs beginning in the 1970's. The "giftedness" was almost exclusively the narrow concept of intelligence, which obviously has been poorly understood. I could see most students lacking in emotional intelligence and social maturity who were accelerated through the left brain curriculum beyond their age peers. These students frequently were socially uncomfortable and in many cases solved this problem by isolating themselves from the general student population. I am not aware of any research on the issue of suicide, but my general observations lead me to believe that gifted students are disproportionately represented in the actual cases of suicide.

Intelligence is one of the five sources of energy which contribute to integrity. When it is developed to the exclusion of any or all of the remaining four sources the individual feels fractured, incomplete and therefore is likely to plunge more deeply into the intellectual development as a way to gain control in his or her life. This only leads to more emotional and social upheaval for them and their families. This great talent of intellect seldom finds a productive role for the benefit of the individual or for the culture.

The development of intelligence, has been the primary focus of educational practices. The emphasis upon left brain learning is a symptom of the closed system. Cultural evolution is at a stand-still until educational efforts are able to accommodate and integrate the multitude of ways people learn into accepted teaching practices. To maintain the present closed educational system, is to further destroy our children and youth. To continue these antiquated practices is unconscionable and immoral.

Chapter Eleven

Emotional Power

It may seem unusual to some, to use the above terminology as the title of this chapter. I have used the terms power and energy interchangeably to soften the sometimes offensive impact of the word power. The word power has taken on a pejorative meaning largely because the closed system reflects the use of power in negative ways. The consequence is to believe all power is negative. Power is the ability to get things done, in an open system this is a positive condition as people are never exploited but rather helped to develop into self-sufficient citizens.

While we are considering the implications behind the use of the word power, I will add more before addressing the *how* of emotional power. During the days of President Nixon's presidency when it became clear that something had been done illegally, with the President's knowledge, the issue of power was frequently debated. It was basically left hanging in the summation contained in a quote from Lord Acton: "Power corrupts and absolute power corrupts absolutely." When Frank Herbert's novel, *Dune* was made into a movie, which I watched, it was apparent he was describing a common power situation.[1] Not long after viewing the movie I read and interview with Herbert in *Psychology today.* The PT interviewer, Ross Stagner asked Herbert if he was in agreement with Lord Acton. Herbert's response was very direct, "That doesn't quite hit the mark. I have a theory that power attracts the corruptible."[2] Herbert went on to explain that power cannot corrupt, it is what people do with power that is corrupt. He said, ". . . those who are attracted to a power position, . . . are those with a predisposition to be corrupted by it."[3]

It is this insight of Herbert's that makes this chapter on emotional power more easily understood. Any power is positive to the extent that it is understood in substance and application. It was said by the Roman historian, Livy, who lived during Christ's time that, "We fear things in proportion to our ignorance of them."[4] It is ignorance, which sets off the negative circumstances out of which people talk. The condition of ignorance leads to acts of corruption. Ignorance and corruption are major indicators of a lack of *integrity*.

The circumstance of lacking intellectual and emotional power leaves the person feeling uneasy and weak. Since they may not be aware that the cause of the weakness is ignorance they tend to be ineffective in their relationships, which tends to make the original condition more deeply felt. Since they are emotionally illiterate they may not know this weakness is the cause of fear. This fear, whether it is consciously identified or not, is the result of being incomplete in some way and life is seeking more completion of them. The sad thing is when the individual strikes out in ways which are harmful to others and especially to themselves without making an effort to alleviate the weakness behind the fear. Fear is perceived as a weakness in the closed system and therefore the enemy and it is to be denied and or defeated at all costs. The open system accepts fear as a gift of creation, an invitation to engage in some self assessment, which can direct thoughts and actions, which will promote growth in preparation for any future unknown. The source of control, all desirable control, in the open system, is internal within the individual.

The presentation of material on emotional energy is discussed at this place in this book because of the great importance this strength has for the individual. It is particularly important to correct Descartes' negative mind set about emotions and feelings.[5] Daniel Goleman in, *Emotional intelligence: why it can matter more than IQ* says that emotions are a guide to situations too important to be left solely to the intellect.[6] He is building on what Aristotle said about managing ones emotional life with intelligence. To not be able to be emotionally in control of one's self, is to have a weakness or a serious lack of integrity.

Returning to Livy's insight, it can be said that being intellectually limited also weakens a person's emotional intelligence or power.[7] These holes in one's potential energy sources, represent not only ignorance but a predilection to corruption. Fear is probably one of the greatest strengths genetically passed on to us from our ancestors. Without fear a person's life is without warning of impending danger. Fear is a gift, an invitation to look at our incompleteness and intelligently look for what is missing, for a life preserving response. The closed system has accepted inappropriate responses out of ignorance, which is completely understandable, but when the ignorance is a preferred state of existence then corruption is prevalent. The open system allows responses from ignorance, also, since it seems impossible for everyone to know everything in every case. The difference is, in the open system, the person is able to gain strength from acting out of ignorance because mistakes are acceptable learning experiences because they decrease ignorance.

Emotional power comes from emotional intelligence. Goleman is using his theoretical base to develop methods of educating people in emotions and feelings.[8] The key element is knowing and accepting one's own feelings. It is impossible to know another's feelings if you do not know them within yourself. The first step seems to be accurate recognition of one's own feelings and then intelligently deciding how to use this energy. For example if you know fear within yourself you can identify it in others and choose to respond in ways which will alleviate the fear. Once the fear is alleviated then something can be done to address the issues behind the fear itself. In this way the emotion of fear has become the vital piece in bringing peace to another person.

Descartes' injunction to discount feelings set the stage for a condition which was worse than neglect.[9] The overt efforts to quash all emotions, particularly in males, has had a heavy cultural cost measured in misery. The emotionally illiterate are ready members of a closed system which believes in punishment or the threat of punishment. Historically, humans have used the ploy of making others more fearful than they themselves feel. The conscious or maybe unconscious motive is that if someone else is more fearful than I, then "I can continue with what I am doing, since they will be so concerned about their survival." This ignorance of the sources of fear makes this person a tyrant.

Many will remember the time Senator Edmund Muskie of Maine was making a bid for the nomination of President of the United States. Someone in the Nixon camp leaked a fictitious letter criticizing Mrs. Muskie. At a news conference, Senator Muskie, openly cried at this deceitful treatment of his wife and himself. I would imagine a great fear or terror went through him that people could be this dishonest and there was no protection against it. The outcome was that his standing in the polls was negatively affected and he was no longer considered a viable candidate. It was his open expression of the emotion by crying in public, which people could not accept from a male. Had he become bellicose and threatened all kinds of retaliation against the perpetrators he would have been more effective in his candidacy. The closed system mentality does not easily accept softness, compromise and forgiveness.

At the beginning of my teaching career it was quite evident that the main disciplinary approach was plenty of fear or more accurately terror. If you could not terrorize a class you were not considered an effective teacher or principal. Then something happened in the 1960's which impacted the use of fear. It was a collective response to the closed system use of fear toward everyone. Teachers organized and began to take stands previously not taken, they were not going to yield to the use of fear. I suspect that students felt this new idea which was loose in the culture. It was the Reality Therapy expert, William Glasser, who discovered that students could no longer be controlled through fear or threat of fear as he reported a new concept in *Schools without failure.*[10] Further development of these ideas by Glasser is found in *Control theory: a new explanation of how we control our lives.*[11] Glasser's impact has been significant in softening the effects of the closed system. Rather than trying to scare children into being good he moved things toward teaching children how to get control in their lives by making better decisions.

The action of Rosa Parks, as a single individual, who refused to sit in the back of the bus where all Blacks were supposed to sit, is also a reflection of this refusal to be controlled by the fear or threat of fear of others. Her emotional intelligence led to others resisting and removing a long standing practice of enforcement of segregation through the use of fear.

There seem to have always been those who choose to hate. This inclination toward hating is rooted in emotional ignorance which produces fear. When I was in Mississippi, I was asked numerous times if I would want a Black person to marry one of my white daughters. This was a response I would get when I would suggest that any citizen living in Mississippi, black or white, should have equal access to the resources of the State, specifically education. I finally understood this line of discourse, since the marriage of one of my daughters to a black person, when they were two and three and a half years of age, had nothing to do with denying Black people the same opportunities as others. The use of this potential circumstance of marriage, was used with me, as it had been with them, to scare me into accepting the status quo and end my line of discussion.

It was America's Henry David Thoreau who pointed out "Nothing is so much to be feared as fear."[12] I believe this reflects an insight into the general lack of the peoples' awarenesses of their emotions in the middle of the nineteenth century, and especially this much needed emotion named fear. It may be a misconception on my part, but I believe Thoreau knew his fear and was not scared by it. It is unclear whether Franklin Delano Roosevelt, in his first presidential inaugural address, was utilizing Thoreau's insight when he said, "The only thing we have to fear is fear itself."[13] Again this was an effort to help people know what their fear is and do something about it rather than react blindly to fear itself. Both Thoreau and Roosevelt were suggesting a degree of emotional intelligence not common within the culture during those respective times, but desperately needed.

The successful instruction in emotional intelligence is based upon recognizing one's own emotions and then being able to accurately identify them in others. This self awareness can be enhanced by assessment. Goleman has utilized the Profile of Nonverbal Sensitivity (PONS) developed by Robert Rosenthal at Harvard to measure people's ability to read the non verbal messages given by others.[14] Goleman has found, as others have found, after testing many individuals, there is, at best, only an incidental relationship between these scores of empathy and IQ tests.[15]

Shame is an emotion of major importance in human cultures. It is closely connected to ethical and moral power. Shame is a sense of regret as the result of not acting with consideration of others. Usually shame is learned from being reproached by one's elders. It is bringing this violation of another's rights or being, to a level of consciousness. It provides a boundary or a limit to what is socially acceptable in particular situations.

When properly learned, the discomfort it brings, alerts one to change his or her direction. Shame works best when it is included in one's considerations of some intended action. Many a junior high student has heard me ask him or her if what he or she is doing or planning to do would make his or her parents proud of them. If one would be ashamed to have his or her parents witness them, then don't do it.

The danger, in the use of shame in helping youth develop, is it can become over used. For the purposes of this section I will call the over use of shame, guilt. The difference between shame and guilt is arbitrary on my part, but necessary to clarify an important distinction involving this deep emotion. Shame is when someone knows they have done something which violates others and they alone know it better than anyone. Guilt is when everyone knows this person has violated the social mores of the culture.

When people refuse to respond to shame, the offended person may feel further violated and then seek some public avenue of redress. I have worked with youth who appear to have no sense of shame, and therefore the use of guilt as a public retribution, to force a feeling of shame, is useless. A fifteen year old boy who would randomly slug someone in the face about every two or three weeks is an example. He was not open to any coercion through the use of guilt nor any rational appeals to stop this behavior. He appeared to not have any shame at all, in effect emotionally illiterate in this area. Things became clearer when his father came in under the prospect of suspension and corroborated the boys behavior. His father said, "I know why he does this. It's because I raised him to be that way. Some people need to be beat up because they are nerds." Three weeks later an older brother was arrested and charged with murder in a contract killing.

The culture has not only relied upon the use of terror but also the use of guilt, to control others in the closed system. As discussed in chapter three, the exploitation of these two emotions - fear and shame - to control others ultimately has the opposite effect. People not only are unable to function but eventually rebel and act out in ways intended to give them a sense of freedom without regard for the welfare of others. More often than not, others are the focus of this acting out.

A person ignorant of fear and shame, in themselves, behave in paradoxical ways. They do not like being controlled by their ignorance, but assume that others are fair game for scaring and shaming, and maybe worse than they experienced. This is again the situation that Freire describes.[16] Those who live under oppression become oppressors and are more oppressive than those from whom they learned. The paradox is cleared up when it can be seen that students of oppression, know no other way to work out their own growth. Obviously the growth is in the negative direction.

A third emotion, which is of importance, to consider is anger. Although there are many emotions, I have chosen these three - fear, shame and anger - as the most worthy of immediate attention. It has been my observation that it is not possible or even necessary to address all the issues of a problem if the key issues can be improved. Improving the key elements of concern always produces improvements in the gestalt of the matter, in this case emotional intelligence.

Anger is a choice, and is most likely to be chosen when a person is feeling the least capable. It is not difficult to understand that a person who is emotionally illiterate, feels out of control most of the time and therefore is always on the defense. Whenever a teacher would complain to me about the behavior of a student and end by saying, "He makes me so angry!", I knew I was working with a person who was emotionally illiterate. The teacher always made the choice to get angry and so would use his or her energy to try to figure out how to get back at the student. One teacher had been fighting with a student, I believed to be gifted, for two thirds of the year, when she decided the boy should be placed in another teacher's class for the remainder of the year. Further, she stipulated that the boy should not only be in this teacher's class, but he should flunk for the whole year, regardless of how well he would do. The teacher was doing the best she could, considering her emotional illiteracy and lack of integrity.

Anger is particularly unproductive in bringing about positive change, since the anger usually puts all other people on guard. Not only does it promote stagnation of growth of all parties involved but it has some definite physical effects upon the angered person. Since the brain is blind to what is really going on out there in the real world, it sends messages to the glands to prepare for the "imagined" danger, the way it does when there is a real danger. When this condition of anger becomes a constant state of being for the person, the body is ready to fight twenty-four hours a day. Redford and Virginia Williams have demonstrated the physical damage to the human body caused by maintaining a constant or nearly constant state of anger in *Anger kills.*[17] They have developed a scale for assessing a person's level of anger or hostility. This Hostility Questionnaire gives a total measure of the three contributing factors, cynicism, anger, and aggression. People with scores of ten or higher, on a scale of forty-six items, have been found to have a significantly higher incidence of heart disease.[18]

Anger, in the sense described by the Williams', is obviously negative and harmful.[19] The emotionally intelligent person will take the earliest indications of anger and determine the cause of this feeling, and usually it is associated with some vague sense of inadequacy. However since the person with constant anger has denied the emotions behind the anger they assume that anger is a primary emotion. Anger is a secondary emotion, one of choice which does not have to be acted upon with negative consequences. The negative use of anger tends to immobilize the person toward positive behaviors. Anger can be used as a signal that the person is feeling inadequate, or helpless. I have found the best way to deal with a tendency to use anger negatively, is to look at the situation and then behave toward the person involved in a helpful way. Making myself helpful to others reduces my sense of helplessness at the source, me. Negative use of anger is always misplaced on what is chosen as the source of one's helplessness, which is external to the individual. The reason for the external orientation is a lack of self awareness and hence emotional illiteracy.

Shame and guilt are two primary emotions which are genetically encoded and anger is a secondary emotion since it is chosen. It has been the negative utilization, of largely these three, which drives the closed system. Emotional intelligence implies the positive handling and use of all emotions, but an important beginning place are these three. The sooner a person begins to use these emotions as the gifts they are, the sooner they can live in the open system because of the increased personal integrity.

Chapter Twelve

Physical Power

Physical power is the most easily recognized of the five sources of power. The very survival of the earliest humans was largely due to physical strength and especially that of the male. This is seen in modern day athletics, shear strength of body is the ultimate in aspirations for many. The sports which developed during the age of games in America have provided an outlet for exceptional physical development. The contests of competition, such as football, boxing, and hockey provide opportunities for the application of "brute" force. Whoever can amass the greatest amount of brute force wins. Other sports activities rely not only on physical abilities but provide opportunities for thinking or outwitting the opponent. The shear display of physical force in these managed activities seems to be the major purpose behind this public exhibition, and at the professional level, the monetary rewards are outstanding. When the contest is over, the winners and losers are always looking for others to dominate with the precision application of force. The question which is left begging is, "What is the socially enduring value of professional athletics?"

Physical ability or power has been relegated to less of a social requirement for shear survival than early humans needed. The nomadic way of life required all people to travel long distances on foot. Any contact with a rival nomadic group or a predatory animal required physical adeptness. Also, the killing of large animals for food purposes, often required considerable physical power before the invention of gun powder. The physically sound body was a necessity and remains so in these days, even without those daily threats to life. War or the threat of war has been the only need for physical soundness of the foot soldier in the twentieth century. The advent of technology and the development of "smart bombs" will require even less physical force. Pushing buttons and flipping toggle switches on a control panel does not require the physical endurance of a foot soldier. As war has developed from the necessity to defend ones possessions and way of life to an overt act of aggressive domination and exploitation of others, what was once hand-to-hand combat with clubs and stones has given way to never seeing or touching those that are to be beaten or destroyed.

So what is the purpose of physical power for the non-combatant? The old adage of "a sound body and a sound mind" can be traced back to the century before Christ when a Roman poet, Horace, wrote, "Grant me, sound of body and of mind. to pass an old age lacking neither honor nor the lyre."[1] The connection between body and mind has been known for many millennia. This aspect of integrity seems not to have escaped the ancients in its importance.

Is a person sound of mind because they had a sound body, or it the other way round? Can a person have one without the other? There are notable examples of people who lived with only one and very limited in the other. The children born with only the brain stem seem to have every physical attribute except all that goes with upper brain function. Usually they do not live long. People have existed in a state of coma for years, some to awaken, and others who eventually die.

A most remarkable example of a person with a sound mind and very limited physical ability is Stephen Hawking. Hawking has lost his ability to walk, talk, and write due to Lou Gehrig's disease, yet with technological devices he is still able to share his immense mental insights into the mysteries of the universe. Hawking in his book, *A brief history of time: from the big bang to black holes*, unlocks and explains the secrets of universe with his mind.[2] He is already considered one of the greatest physicists of the twentieth century.

To return to the question of whether a person can exist without one or the other, body or mind, the answer seems to be no. People classified as idiots often live for extended periods of time with strong physical power and are sometimes called an "ox" because they are little more than a beast of burden. The person with a ravaged physical body, such as Hawking, is considered a brilliant mind. These two sources of power, the physical and mental or intellectual, apparently require the presence of the other at least to a minimum degree. The effects of the reduced presence of one has a limiting effect upon the individual which vary from individual to individual. The presence of some degree of physical power along with some degree of intellectual power contribute to integrity.

The physical body is a phenomenal receptor of information. The studies done of the children, placed in institutions at birth, indicate the importance of contact for new-borns with mothers or mother substitutes. Spitz reported, in 1945, severe mental retardation of institution reared children.[3] The orphans of the former nation of Yugoslavia are presenting the symptoms of a lack of human contact, they have failed to develop in many ways. This has been a very unexpected trauma for some of the American adoptive parents. Some of these children seem unable to process what is rational and socially acceptable. The deprivation of human contact in the first few years of life is critical to the development of mental capabilities for effective socialization.

The body continues throughout life to be a receptor of information, not only from the external world but internally as well. The physical body functions like a giant bulletin board, all internal conditions are monitored and therefore available to the awareness of the individual.

Starvation is an internal state which is painfully delivered. The invasion of the body by organisms or foreign objects is telegraphed to the bulletin board. The sense of touch, temperature, wetness or dryness, and pressure all are part of the signals which convey important information for the safety and comfort of the body.

As mentioned in chapter 10, when a person believes there is an external danger to themselves, this causes the pituitary gland to signal the brain and chemicals are released in the blood stream which prepare the body for fighting of fleeing. When people have not developed a keen sense of the biochemical reactions within their bodies they are unable to translate any of the symptoms accurately. A person who gets scared and then becomes angry may not notice the change in the taste in his or her mouth or the quickening of the pulse or a flushing of the face or excessive perspiration.

These bodily reactions to fear, when not utilized to curtail the negative response to fear, usually develop into psychosomatic conditions. The auto-immune system may either stop functioning or become over-active to the stress the person feels. This contributes to conditions such as diabetes, some forms of arthritis, some forms of skin eruptions, respiratory problems, panic attacks, headaches, back or neck aches. I suggest reading *Who gets sick: how beliefs, moods, and thoughts affect your health*, written by Blair Justice, for well documented evidence of the connection between body and mind.[4]

Justice's explanations, based on numerous studies, indicate the negative affect upon a healthy body from negative thoughts and beliefs.

It is now a rare person that becomes ill, from the effects of invading germs. The vast majority of illnesses are now the result of mental processes which negatively impact the physical body. The reductionistic approach to traditional medicine treats the body as a separate entity. This approach relies upon medicating the patient with a chemical to get the physical body back in chemical balance. Giving people placebos instead of the medicine they are told they are getting quite often gets the same results as those who receive the medicine. The placebo effect is the smoking gun of the connection between the health of the body and the mind.

Biofeedback is a process where a person is aware of what is happening in his or her body. The beneficial effect of biofeedback is that a person can become more closely attuned to what is happening in his or her body and keep it going, if it is beneficial, or shut it down, if it detrimental. It has been demonstrated that people can be taught how to warm up the extremities of their arms and legs by thinking about more blood going to them. One woman was able to loose a tumor by thinking she was sending little Pac Man like creatures to the tumor through her blood stream. This deeper level of body knowing and awareness gives the person greater power with his or her body.

In my own life I have had the experience of having a pituitary tumor surgically removed through a microscopic surgical procedure. There is no way that it can be shown that this tumor was the result of a suppressed immune system as no testing was done to verify these conditions. However there is evidence in the scientific field, that suggests, from time to time, all people probably produce a few cancerous cells. The T-cells in a healthy body are always on the lookout for "foreign" cells and will attack them before a tumor develops, hence leaving the person essentially cancer free. The presence of a tumor on my pituitary gland coincides with an extremely stressful time in my professional career and could be the result of a weakened immune system. Another symptom during those stressful times, was excessive weight gain. Both are examples of my past inability to effectively respond to the source of the stress, due to my lack of self-awareness. Recent MRI's, CAT scans, and X-rays gave the examining doctor, who monitors my condition, a reason to ask, "Are you sure you had surgery?" He jokingly said that he could see no signs of the surgery, which had been done fifteen years earlier.

Exercise and nutrition are aspects of physical power. Within the limits of the ability and age of the person, exercise is important but not in the same way it was to people a hundred years ago or longer. Then, exercise was more a necessity to carry out the required daily routines of the culture. Before the automobile, people either walked or rode a horse or in a wagon pulled by a horse or other beast of burden. The people, who settled the western part of the United States, who came in covered wagons, did not need to do a daily exercise regime to stay physically healthy. Today, with the automobile and television, may children are at risk of growing into adulthood in poor physical condition, because of the sedentary life style available to them. Having worked in junior high schools, I am still concerned about the number of children who can not lift their own body, doing a two armed pull-up. This is surely not a good situation for a healthy body.

Nutrition is a major concern since the essential way the body receives the materials it needs to grow and repair itself is through eating. When the essential building materials are not available some part of the body is in danger of insufficient development. A major part of the body which can suffer from a lack of proper diet is the brain. The condition where children endure great starvation and live are mentally impaired as adults in spite of the genetic predisposition to be otherwise. A child living through starvation has a lower IQ than he or she would have had with an adequate diet.

The children and adults living with abundant food supplies usually do not starve. One exception, is the person who chooses not to eat, or to get the food out of his or her body as quickly as possible, by either purging or the use of laxatives. This behavior can lead to death if carried to extreme. The reasons behind anorexia and bulimia are not fully understood but generally are considered the result of a lack of self-esteem or a sense of being un-important to others, who should care about them. The beliefs behind self-induced starvation need more attention and earlier intervention even before the symptoms become blatantly evident. It was first thought this was a female problem but it has now been shown that males also are included in this syndrome.

Overeating is currently the epidemic which consumes huge amounts of efforts to combat it. A recent study, which had broad coverage in the media, indicated the effectiveness of "weightloss" programs are only effective with about five percent of people. Although a person on a given program may achieve the desired weight loss, within a year or two, ninety-five percent of them regain the weight, often with some added gain. The major contributor to the failure of these programs is, the program does not include anything about why the person overeats, or if this factor is presented, the participants do not make the connection. The success in the dieting phase works because the people **do** what they are **told**. As soon as the dieting phase ends, and they stop doing what they have been told, the eating habits return. People who are not aware of why they eat, and are over weight, eat for other reasons than just nutrition.

Insights into why people overeat are found in a book written by Geneen Roth, *When food is love: exploring the relationship between eating and intimacy.*[5] Roth points out that overeating is an act of desperation.[6] We are compulsive about eating when we have something to hide, something we fear more than overeating or being overweight. In some ways we are protecting a wound which gives us some sense of intimacy and food gives us a way to protect this wound and also feel some sense of love.

Another more recent book is *Make the connection: ten steps to a better body and a better life,* co-authored by Bob Greene and Oprah Winfrey which gives important clues as to why we eat more than we need and a plan for changing beliefs.[7] The beliefs are all about us and what is really important and how we can use food as nutrition instead of as a substitute for intimacy or a protector against our worst fears.

Physical power can be developed and maintained through proper nutrition and exercise. Skills in biofeedback and emotional intelligence help in identifying our dominate and prevailing feelings about food intake and exercise.

Chapter Thirteen

Moral Power

Hutchins believed moral development was a parental responsibility.[1] This seems defensible since parents are the first influences in the child's life, before the child goes to school, or ventures very far outside of the family circle. A child who learns right and wrong early in life has an advantage in all other areas of development. The ability to choose a socially acceptable behavior is a very powerful and desirable skill.

Moral power and ethical power are generally synonymous for the sake of discussion here. There seems to be evidence of gender implications in the use of these terms. Any male who digresses from the cultural norm is said to be unethical while a female who may commit the same error is said to be immoral. The distinction is that to be immoral is to have some permanent character flaw while being unethical means the person has only done a wrong in that instance. The closed system attitude gives this advantage to men and withholds the same from females.

Moral and ethical power are much more than being virtuous. Virtue is an indicator of one's being moral or ethical. Virtue does not stand alone against the world of choices but is held in balance with the vices which are part of the same continuum. Aristotle described virtue as choosing between "too much" and "not enough" of something. When the seven deadly sins are examined, they can be placed on the same continuum as the virtues.

Gluttony, one of the seven deadly sins, is eating too much good food. Starvation, on the other hand, is a vice because food is being withheld. It is this balance which determines virtue. The choices which place the person somewhere between *excess* and *defect* represent the *"means between two extremes."* This medial averageness is said to make a person virtuous.

William Bennett in his attempts to bring about a correctness of behavior in the American culture, wrote *The book of virtues: a treasury of great moral stories.*[2] Bennett's book received wide acclaim. as it appeals to many who want to return to the "good old days" of imagined virtue. The moral tales he included are representative of many which I heard when I was growing up. My frustration was then, as it is now, "Why do people who claim to be virtuous act in such vicious ways?" It doesn't seem that the issue of being with virtue or vice is a black and white issue. Vicious and vice come from the same root word *(vitium)* which means fault or wickedness. Virtue comes from the root word *(virtus)* which means man, therefore a male moral excellence. There obviously was some attempt at identifying virtue as the more desirable of the two.

For some, all of the injunctions against certain immoral acts seem to fall on deaf ears and unwilling hearts. This condition came to full bloom for me during the seventies when Nixon and Agnew were campaigning for the presidency and vice presidency of the United States. They both extolled the virtues of "law and order" while being a party to illegal activities in their lives. Agnew was accused of income tax evasion and receiving kick-backs from contractors while he was Governor of Maryland. He pled no contest to the income tax charge and resigned as vice president. The burglary of the Democratic Party headquarters in the Watergate building was a vicious act, which resulted in Nixon resigning the presidency.

The strength of virtue is in the reliance upon choices made by the individual. Aristotle associated more significance to enlightened conscience than obedience to the rules, such as divine command and Kant's categorical imperative. A weakness of the virtue ethics is, "How does a person decide just how honest to be." What is the mean between the two extremes of total honesty and total dishonesty? What is the mean between being good and bad? Are honesty and good, two virtues which have no means? Given a choice, not very many people would choose to associate with the dishonest and bad person. Is it possible for a person to be too honest and too good? If so, should they seek a mean between these two extremes? How is this mean to be determined?

Robert Hutchinson has published a book, as an attempt to bring a more realistic perspective to *The book of virtue*. Hutchinson believes virtue cannot exist without the existence of vice as detailed in *The book of vices*.[3] In some cases, a little vice might be better for the person striving to be virtuous. Aristotle believed that too much virtue is in fact a form of vice. This can become a reality when the somber promoters of virtue are able to get laws passed which allow the government to control the individual citizen's freedom of choice. The interference in private citizen's life, in the United States, is considered the rightful domain of the individual and the government should stay out of it. Virtuousness is often claimed by both sides of the political ideologies and is neither right nor left, but rather excess which makes it a vice.

An important theory of moral development was conceived by the late Lawrence Kohlberg.[4] Kohlberg's great contribution to an area of study, previously excluded or left at the margins of study, was demonstrating that moral development could be empirically studied and philosophically consistent. His stage developmental theory has led to further studies particularly in assessment of moral development.

Carol Gilligan in, *In a different voice: psychological theory and women's development* presents research and arguments that men and women develop differently in many ways including morally.[5] Measurements of moral development are based upon the male theories of male development and largely disregard the female aspects. It is obvious that male and females are socialized differently - females are to have things fixed and males are supposed to fix things as an example. Whether these differences can be accommodated in the assessments of moral development is yet to be worked out.

James Rest has developed the *Defining Issues Test* (DIT) based upon Kohlberg's theories but with some changes.[6] Where Kohlberg believed every person advances through a linear sequence of moral development, Rest believes moral development is the result of specific situations. *The Defining Issues Test(DIT)*, developed by Rest, contains six moral dilemmas to which a respondent selects from a set of possible considerations, each reflects levels of moral functioning, those which support a choice of behavior.[7] The reader is directed to *Moral development: advances in research and theory* by Rest for greater depth of information.[8]

Rest believes the only consistent correlation with increased levels of moral functioning is the level of formal education.[9] He has found no correlation with gender, age, ethnicity, race or socio-economic status. Gilligan's concern about gender differences does not hold up in the results reported by Rest. Over a ten year period of administering the DIT to mixed groups I found no reason to disagree with Rest's reported findings. In fact it is just as likely that women will score higher than men on this measure. If there are differences between the genders, it may be more in the process of arriving at a decision and not so much what the decision is. I am not aware of any studies of how women and men may process information in the task of arriving at a moral decision.

As an educator and a professor of education, the greatest concern that I have had is the level of moral functioning of educators in comparison with those they teach. As a principal, I worked with staff members who sold drugs to students, did drugs with students, bought drugs from students, sneaked beer into a school dance for the students, had sex with students and conspired with students to keep the truth from being discovered by the parents and administration. These kinds of problems are not what any parents want to have develop where they are sending their children to schools. When asked, parents will express hope that all adults will be of a higher level of moral functioning than their children.

Adults or anyone of higher moral functioning are the only ones who can induce moral development in children and youth. The person at a higher level of moral functioning understands the moral functioning of those at a lower level and encourages them to move to a higher level. The person at the lower level of moral functioning does not understand the higher level of moral functioning and will resist moving to the higher level and is therefore stressed by the social expectations he or she encounters. A variation of this is represented in the situation of high moral functioning high school students rarely being elected class president or most popular.

In recent years a "general studies" requirement for senior level students was put in place at Chadron State College. All students are required to successfully complete a course in ethics. The classes, with which I was associated, were pre-tested with the DIT at the beginning of the semester and post tested at the end of the semester. The usual change in mean score was about seven points higher. This change is consistent with what can be expected. These results were reported at the National Ethics Conference in Long Beach California.[11]

One argument against the DIT, is that it can be manipulated. My experience indicates manipulation results in lower scores, but never higher scores. One of the reasons this may happen is that the test contains nonsense items which do not count although they may sound lofty. I think the primary reason the scores go up is because most people are not satisfied when they receive their pre-test scores and work at understanding moral and ethical reasoning. Most people believe they have been helped by the experience of formal education in ethics and they look at the world in different ways.

To return to the sigmoid curve first presented in chapter 3, it is possible to plot the six stages of Kohlberg's theory on the curve. Figure 13-1 indicates that Stage one functioning is based upon deference to authority. At this stage the person is totally reliant upon some outside authority to provide the choices. In the older religions and some of the newer religious groups, deference to the authority of the groups leader is enforced. The unquestioning compliance of the commands are couched to reflect the divine command of the God being worshipped. David Koresh of the Waco, Texas, "Branch Davidians" was an example of people functioning at stage one. This is probably true for the followers of Marshall Applewhite and the cult called "Heaven's Gate."

Stage two functioning is based upon acting in one's self interest. The ethical studies of traditional philosophy describe this as "ethical egoism." The dictum is, "I should do whatever pleases me and others should do what pleases me." It can be compared with a trial adventure into freedom of choice, but without regard for the effects upon others. Acting in one's self interest without regard for the interests of others, is the source of much conflict and misery in the world. Not much awareness is reflected in what happens internally, since the actions are based upon getting what is "out there" for oneself.

Stage three functioning is associated with conformity and compliance, based upon pleasing others. This is that delightful age when children want to be good girls and good boys and will yield to nearly all requests of those older. This is no problem when the requests reflect high moral considerations. Children are very productive,

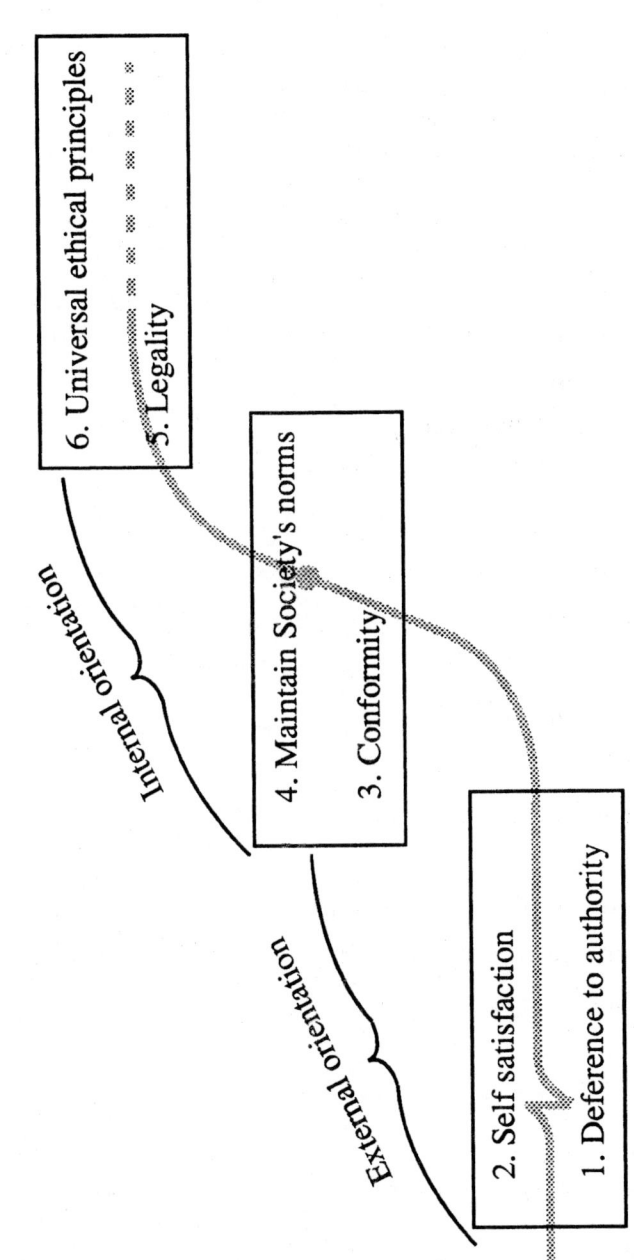

Figure 13.1
MORAL DEVELOPMENT CURVE

especially the intermediate grade level students, in their school work. They work to please their parents and the teachers. A danger exists in that children can not readily discern when something being asked of them is immoral. Often this is when incest occurs and children are recruited for pornographic exploitation. Rather than displease those asking things of them, they will do it, apparently without too much thought. The major thought is centered around whether it was done well enough to please.

The brackets indicate that Stages one, two and three are more externally oriented than the last three stages. This represents a lack of freedom for the individual when they function at these levels. The source of control for the choices is seen to be outside of the person and has a limiting effect upon them. Some people may live their entire lives in these lower levels and probably have feelings of being controlled but not really knowing what to do about it. The stage two person who gets caught doings things that are immoral rarely sees anything wrong with what they did. "The problem is getting caught."

Stages four, five and six are more internally oriented and reflect more consideration for the effect upon others and themselves. A stage four person is primarily concerned about maintaining the social norms for their own sake. These people express great satisfaction in being able to perpetuate the status quo.

Reflecting on my experiences in Mississippi, during the forced integration of Ole Miss, I am reminded that most natives of Mississippi could justify the attempts at continued segregation with the adage, "When in Rome, do as the Romans do."

Stage five moral functioning is based upon following the law and avoiding court action. There is little problem with this level when the laws are a true reflection of ethics and morals. One doesn't have to look too far to find examples of laws or actions taken, based upon some laws which are immoral. The nineteenth amendment, to the U.S. Constitution granting suffrage to women, ended an immoral practice of not allowing women the right to vote. This practice was based upon the notion that women are property and therefore will do what their husbands tell them so they do not need to vote. Some states have had laws which did not allow women to inherit their husbands wealth at the time of his death. The rationale for this law was also based upon the notion of women being property of the male. "After all, it is pretty ridiculous to believe property can inherit property."

Stage six functioning is based upon what Kohlberg referred to as "Universal Ethical Principles." This is similar to Kant's categorical imperative in that there are principles that go beyond law that guide what a person does. These principles reflect concern for not only the actor but those who will be affected by the choice. There simply are some things that must be done and other things which should never be done. People at this stage are deeply aware of the hard work to get to this level and to maintain this level of functioning. Given the alternatives, they will choose the hard work and threats to them for functioning at this level. These people are not controlled externally but are so self aware and well integrated they have the courage to exist in the face of great danger. The purpose of their life is defined by living by these principles and encouraging others to do likewise.

The development of moral power, initially, is begun in the home. To the extent that a foundation is formed in childhood, a person will have an easy or hard time making decisions of right and wrong. The lower moral functioning people have a difficult time understanding the higher moral functioning reasoning. This difficulty in understanding produces cognitive dissonance which can propel the lower functioning person to move to a higher level of moral functioning. The higher moral functioning people have a moral and ethical responsibility to display the higher ethical reasoning and behavior. This task of moving to the highest levels of morality is not easy.

Chapter Fourteen

Spiritual Power

Spiritual power is being presented as the last center of energy for the reason that without spirit a person is little more than a hollow or empty vessel. Spirit is the power which blends with the other four centers of energy and renders them positive and useful. An early effort in searching for this deficiency in myself led me to M. Scott Peck's book *The road less traveled: a new psychology of love, traditional values and spiritual growth.*[1] Peck defines love as, "The will to extend oneself for the purpose of nurturing one's own or another's spiritual growth."[2] I have expanded this understanding for myself to include the unconditional regard for others as well as myself. I am who I am, and it is important to love myself so that I can love others. My experiences suggest that a person who cannot accept themselves as a gift to the world does not have the spiritual energy see others as gifts in the world.

Another important insight, for me, was what I found in Jerry Jampolsky's book called *Love is letting go of fear.*[3] I struggled with this concept for sometime, first believing that fear was a weakness and letting go meant not being afraid. It helped me realize that I had been scared all my life, but spent my spiritual energy largely in denying my fear. The breakthrough is that fear is a gift as discussed in chapter ten. Fear is a gift that something needs more of my attention than I have given it. As a gift, fear is an invitation to find ways to help others in ways that benefit them. The practice of ignoring fear, leads a person to do those things which are deemed important to them without regard for the needs of others. This leads to a nasty situation of doing things "to" others instead of acting out of love which is doing things "with" others.

Love cannot be hoarded but it can be withheld from oneself and others. Love grows to the extent that it is freely given away. It grows within the one doing the giving and it grows within others and the culture. This is contrary to the Newtonian laws of thermodynamics. The positive energy of love represents and increase in energy in the world and therefore violates the law that all energy is dissipated and therefore lost to the universe. The old law basically said that all energy systems are "down hill." Prigogine demonstrated that energy systems that seem to be in chaos are more accurately in a state of moving to higher energy levels.[4] This is the case for spirituality as it continues to increase in the culture and the world.

Choosing to act out of love due to the invitation of fear is possible to the extent that the person is alive in the present moment. In parts one and two I discussed the effect of allowing guilt and terror to dominate one's life. When guilt and terror rule a person's life, his or her sense of the present moment is weak and possibly non-existent. It is the positive choices of acceptance and love which expand the sense of the present moment. When people live in the past, out of guilt, and in the future, in a state of terror, they miss the event of their life. Life is a journey into greater power and fulfillment, not being stuck in the past and/or future; no one can control the past or future. It is rather the acceptance of one's self and experiences, and a strong sense of hope, which makes the power of the well integrated person available to live freely and spontaneously in the present. Choosing to live out of guilt and in terror consumes all the person's energy and leads to a limited and stagnated life.

Spirituality is the power which is responsible for the sense of soul. Soul is the embodiment of the power from all five centers of power as they are activated and regulated through the spiritual. I believe spiritual power is central to the existence of the person. It is the spiritual power which brings the energy of the other four energies to the present. The individual has control over the use of the spiritual power and can use it for negative as well as positive purposes. When the person chooses, that is uses moral power, to send the spiritual power on negative errands of the past, the energy reserves of the individual are depleted. The person feels weakened and the spiritual power, in that negative place, is not available for loving since it is attached to negativity. Letting go of the wounds of the past or the fear of future wounds, such as Jampolsky recommended, allows the spiritual side to be manifested in the form of soul.

The weakened souls of many adolescents are the causes of all the problems typically associated with the teenage years. Little thought is given to these "problems" and therefore they are not seen as the symptoms of a lack of development of the soul. Many of these youth feel life has passed them by at the onset of the teenage years. Some of them tell us they feel dead and some adults scoff at them, not knowing what the problem is.

The spiritual growth of the individual is the proper domain of the Church. As Hutchins pointed out, when the church takes over the responsibility of intellectual development and moral development they often leave the spiritual development un-attended.[5] Intellectual and moral power without spiritual power at best leave the individual with a weakened soul and therefore a lack of courage. Each new life is an adventure and requires courage to live and grow. The spirit gives us a stronger sense of soul which is needed for this journey.

Joseph Campbell's life of exploring the myths of all peoples has been recorded and provides insights into the value of myths in achieving soulful living. Campbell, in *An open life: Joseph Campbell in Conversation with Michael Toms*, (edited by Maher and Briggs) insists that myths are not untruths nor are they facts.[6] They are metaphors which go beyond fact and actually inform the fact. Myth comes from deep insights out of the spiritual when a person may realize something for the first time. Myths have guided our ancestors for centuries in the absence of fact and have contributed to the discovery of facts.

The creation of humans is a mystery. To understand that life is a mystery does not take away from the creation but protects it from the damage that is done when people try to control the mystery. A controlled mystery will probably not move in the direction of the mystery's plan. Life as a mystery is to be lived and experienced to its fullest. Humans are created with the power tools to live a life of mystery and it is out of living this mystery that one gains fulfillment, purpose, joyfulness and serenity.

James Hillman, in *The soul's code: in search of character and calling*, asserts that "The soul of each of us is given a unique daimon before we are born, and it has selected an image or pattern that we live on earth." "A calling may be postponed, avoided, intermittently missed. It may also possess you completely. Whatever; eventually it will out. It makes it claim. The daimon does not go away."[7] This kernel of the soul, which Hillman calls a daimon, is what makes each human different from each other human. I believe this kernel, or essential part of the soul, can find expression through the soul more easily, when people have integrity and are not ashamed or fearful of what the kernel may be pushing them to do.

People are wired to seek a sense of soul for themselves. It seems rather remote that a person can achieve a strong sense of soul in total isolation from others. It also seems remote that a person who is forced or obligated to associate with people who have little soul, will develop much sense of soul. The human is created with the "wiring" which calls for soul development. I believe all misery of the world is indirectly and directly related to the lack of soul development. I am aware of some who, because of great soulfulness, who have been persecuted and punished for having this quality. I believe most people are more afraid of pain than of dying. The person with a strong soul will fear neither and therefore not contribute to the acts against them. The very soulful person will actually take the negative energy of anyone attacking them, transform it and return it as a positive gift of love.

Spiritual power not only leads to a fuller development of soul but removes the individual from acting out the charade of victimization. People who are week spiritually use victimization as a way to gain intimacy and control as explained by Caroline Myss, in *Why people don't heal: how you can overcome the hidden blocks to wellness.*[8] Creating a life of victimhood is a choice, therefore a moral decision, and the closed system encourages victimhood from generation to generation. The victim lacks strength of integrity from a lack of development in all five areas of power. Playing the game of victim perpetuates this stagnation of development by tying up all of the limited energy. This then results in the person being miserable and making everyone else miserable.

An area of critical cultural concern is providing the appropriate environment for the rearing of children. Having sexual intercourse and or getting married, because society may prefer it that way, does not in and of itself provide the appropriate environment. The appropriate environment is best produced when both parents make a commitment, first to their own growth and development in all five areas, secondly to each other and the children which are produced. People with underdeveloped souls are unable to make a lasting commitment to others since they have not been successful in making a commitment to their own growth and development. A person is only able to share what they have in themselves.

The lack of soulful development of youth is a serious problem for society, with more and more adolescent females choosing to keep their babies born out of wedlock. Children having babies does not meet the requirement of an appropriate environment. This is further complicated by the reason some of the girls choose to keep their babies, "so they will have someone to love them." These new born children are expected to deliver their mothers from their lives as victims. Quite the opposite happens, the new mother is further victimized, the newborn is a victim and learns the ways of victimhood.

Many years ago, it is my understanding, the word *lazy* literally meant a dislike for some activity. When this concept is applied to self development of one's sources of power it takes on quite a different meaning than comes from the Puritan work ethic. Lazy came to mean, not working hard at accumulating material wealth. This may have been an early motivator to unite people behind the industrial revolution. ". . .the Lord rewards him according to his works." (Second Timothy, 4-14) as it was translated in the King James version.[9] This interpretation of scripture promoted effort more toward efficiency than toward intimacy.

During my elementary years of schooling we were encouraged to be good citizens through the organization of the Young Citizens League (YCL). Through YCL, we learned parliamentary procedure as well as self-sufficiency in taking care of ourselves and the school classroom. We learned the rudimentary skills of being collaborative and supportive. When I became a teacher in the late fifties, emphasis was switched to being a good consumer and away from citizenship. Efficiency and consumerism are two forces which destroy intimacy and the development of the soul.

Thomas Moore in *Soul mates: honoring the mysteries of love and relationships* states, "Spirit and soul are absolutely necessary to human life, they are not identical."[10] Without soul, commitment or bonding is impossible. The soul lives in the crevices of one's being while the aspects of spirit, intellect, physical, moral and emotions are more clearly visible. Hillman likens the soul to an acorn, which hides the true nature of the oak tree. The essence of the oak is hidden but resides in the hidden depths of the acorn only to be awakened under the right conditions.[11]

The spiritual core of integrity is the critical force in developing courage and soul. The soul delivers messages to the person's being which require responses from the person. Response to the soul's urgings or code, are more likely to occur when the person has courage and the power of integrity to act in harmony with these soulful messages.

PART FOUR

ACHIEVING LIFE'S POTENTIAL THROUGH INTEGRITY

"I know no safe depository of the ultimate powers of society but the people themselves, and if we think them not enlightened enough to exercise their control with a wholesome discretion, the remedy is not to take it from them but to inform their discretion by education." (Thomas Jefferson)

"Hero worship is strongest where there is least regard for human freedom." (Herbert Spencer)

"Our civilization is still in the middle stage: scarcely beast, in that it is no longer wholly guided by instinct; scarcely human, in that is not yet wholly guided by reason." (Theodore Dreiser)

"One man cannot do right in one department of life while he is occupied in doing wrong in any other department. Life is one indivisible whole." (Mahatma Gandhi)

"There is an urgent need, around the world, for leadership by strong ethical persons - those who by nature are disposed to be servants (in the sense of helping others to become healthier, wiser, freer, more autonomous and more likely themselves to be servants) and who therefore can help others to move in constructive directions. Servant-leaders are healers in the sense of making whole by helping others to a larger and nobler vision and purpose than they would be likely to attain for themselves. (Robert Greenleaf)

This is the concluding section to the book and extends beyond the why, what and how of the previous three sections. Part four provides information for answering the question of *IF*. If one has integrity will things improve for them and the culture?

Many persons over the centuries have conceptualized the possibilities for improved cultural evolution. Many of these ideas have contained prejudiced perceptions for guidance, which have been reinforced by praise and punishment, and thus perpetuate the closed system.

The open system will come about in fuller form to the extent that people with the will to act out of love, encouragement, and discipline exert this positive energy in the world. The reality of the culture will be transformed when a critical mass of people act on their perception that to be more fully human is to be loving and compassionate.

When the heroes of society become those of great integrity instead of those who have sought to be a hero by accomplishing some physically demanding feat, a more valuable resource will have been placed before our youth as authentic role models. It is not realistic for our youth to worship the heroes of entertainment and professional athletics because of the very nature of competition. In the open system each and everyone has the opportunity to become a bona fide hero in their own right, as they display a courageous soul through achieving integrity.

Chapter Fifteen

The Realization of Freedom

Freedom has long been sought by people from many previous generations. The matter becomes one of "freedom from" and/or "freedom to." Or could it be both? The term liberty contains the element of freedom. What is the implication for the person who has liberty or has been liberated? Liberation suggests that a condition of being held hostage has existed. In this case freedom means being free from being held against one's will. Is it the will which is seeking freedom? Is the will the essence of the soul? Is the soul being held captive? If the person, or the will, or the soul is being held captive, who or what is holding it captive? What is the cause of a sense of a lack of freedom or liberty?

It seems apparent that a lack of integrity within the person is a prime factor in the lack of freedom. Therefore the solution to this lack of freedom, is to develop a higher level of integrity within each person. The closed system has operated to control people in ways which interfere in the development of integrity. The removal of these negative, controlling mechanisms will not result in increased integrity unless they are replaced by positive, liberating mechanisms. The closed system methods are so endemic in the culture, that it is hard to imagine anyone escaping all of the negative influence. Therefore, at this time in the evolution of the cultures, it is necessary to carry on a two part effort to achieve freedom. The first part requires learning about the negative traits which have been thoroughly taught and learned by individuals to varying degrees so they can accept, this is the way they are. The second part requires learning the positive counter-parts, which will promote the growth and development of integrity.

The youth with whom I have worked have continually demonstrated how quickly both of these tasks can be accomplished, sometimes in a split second. A common situation in junior high schools is name calling. One student calls another a "chicken" or something worse. In any case it is something, which if it were true, would be a serious character flaw. At the level of development of the early adolescent, where they are trying to establish an identity, this treatment by others is an assault on their integrity and identity. The usual response is usually physical, a fist in the face or hair pulling and kicking.

My intuition has told me for many years that these youth really do not want to fight. They only fight because the closed system has taught them this, as an acceptable response, to save their honor. Yet they always feel degraded, and especially those who were the victors. It is this sense of a loss of power and dignity. which makes them receptive to alternatives. After I would gain their trust and their permission to share my perceptions of them, with them, they would listen and discover a new response to these personal attacks.

Typically I would begin with a statement of how important it seemed to them to maintain their dignity and to be in control of themselves. It was a rare student who did not agree with this perception of himself or herself. At this level of congruence, it was then possible to say something like, "You want to be in control, don't you?" They would readily agree. Then I would ask, "Who has control when someone calls you a name?" Usually only a short pause was necessary for them to see that the person calling them the name had the control. And finally I would ask them, "How do they get this control?" To which the student would display a slight grin and say, "I guess I gave them the control." At this point the matter was easily resolved by discussing ways to not give your power away and stay in control.

We knew we had been successful when we would overhear statements in the hallway like the following. "I know you want to get into a fight, but it is not worth it in this school, because we will both be suspended and I am here to learn, not to see how many people I can get into a fight with." This student had not only learned the power of self-control but was in effect teaching it to other students. This would not have been possible without the consistent enforcement of rules about fighting. These students always felt more free and therefore more safe than previously. A school, in which the positive energy of the open system flows, is a safe community for everyone.

John Dewey in *Freedom and Culture* argued that to call a society a democracy may not be accurate, since citizens may be denied their guaranteed freedom the same as in a totalitarian state.[1]

> . . .we need to examine every one of the phases of human activity to ascertain what effects it has in release, maturing and fruition of the potentialities of human nature. . . .Find out how all the constituents of our culture are operating and then see to it that whenever and wherever needed they be modified in order that their workings may release and fulfill the possibilities of human nature.[2]

Freedom and liberty mean being able to develop oneself and therefore have advantages the individual will never be able to realize if left to fend for himself or herself. People come into the world with little advantage, that is they are essentially dependent upon others for their own survival as well as growth and development. In other words each person much be given advantage as a birth right - they can get it no other way. When societal and political efforts are directed in this manner, the full potential of human nature of the citizens is released.

Advantage means having something of value - both material and non-material - food and love. One without the other is valueless in the long term. As people receive these advantages the next question becomes "What to do with them?" Many have mistakenly hoarded them, which is of no value at best and damaging at worst. The only reasonable purpose of advantage, is to live a life of the fullest realization of one's potential; the willful exercise of freedom.

The person who gains great advantage in his or her lifetime may do it one of two ways - by taking advantage of others or by giving advantage to others. The former method of gaining advantage is tyranny and is not in the best interest of anyone, not even the tyrant.

The great challenge of today is to move human effort toward the realization that true advantage is giving it away; not hoarding it, keeping it away from others, or *taking* advantage of others. Since a rewarding life seems to require advantages, and all people seek rewards in their lives, the solution is to make sure everyone gets advantages from those who are more highly endowed with advantage. If this were the common circumstance, I believe that as people mature and age, they will have more advantage than anyone and those just beginning the life journey would receive this needed advantage. There seems to be only one true purpose for gaining advantage, and that is to give it to those without as much advantage. To be free is to not only have advantage, but free to give it away.

It is unreasonable to expect the less mature to be able to make many great contributions to themselves or others without first gaining advantage. At first glimpse this seems to be very much like a parasitic relationship.

In fact some have described the developing fetus as a parasite. However with a long range view, one can see the relationship is truly symbiotic in that the senior members of society are compelled by the abundance of advantage to put it to the best use possible. The best use is to give it away to those without advantage. Advantage not given away becomes a burden and destroys the recipient or holder of the original advantage.

It is incumbent upon those with advantage to give it away, not only to free the current holder of advantage of the burden, but to let it take root in a new life and in a new time. When advantage is generously passed on to each succeeding generation, at least three new advantages are gained. First, the advantage is maintained from generation to generation - possibly improved upon and second, the people giving away the advantage have the fullest benefit of it, and third, new advantages may be created which enhance the lives of both generations and all future generations.

To be a leader is to give away all the advantages you have. These advantages were planted in you as a fertile environment for this gift of life and therefore each person's duty is to pass the advantages on to each new generation.

History is an excellent example of what happens when those with advantage withhold advantage from others and hoard what advantage they have justly or more than likely unjustly gained. This always leads to the insanity of war, where the true and most desirable alternative should be compassion. Einstein, in reflecting upon the cultural expressions of freedom concluded:

> In war it serves that we may poison and mutilate each other. In peace it has made our lives hurried and uncertain. Instead of freeing us in great measure from spiritually exhausting labor, it has made men into slaves of machinery, who for the most part complete their monotonous long days work with disgust and must continually tremble for their poor rations.[3]

Freedom is gained to the extent that a person is able to overcome the ignorance with which we all come into this world. When the advantages given to the elders of the culture are not abundantly shared with the youngest members, everyone loses the freedom that everyone seeks. Freedom is knowing everything that is possible to know, and being able to use it in positive and helpful ways. Ignorance is not anything a person should be ashamed of, but should understand that the more ignorance they carry the less free they will be. The only form of ignorance of which a person should be ashamed of is, the ignorance of his or her own ignorance. This profound ignorance leads to misery and suffering since these people do not feel free and often see others with freedom, as having taken theirs from them. Ignorance leads to fanaticism and hatred.

Freedom can become a burden to those who choose to remain ignorant. These people may seek relief by trying to escape the heavy responsibility that comes with freedom. Erich Fromm, in writing about the German response to freedom, of seeking totalitarianism instead, asserts in *Escape from freedom*

> ...that man, the more he gains freedom in the sense of emerging from the original oneness with man and nature and the more he becomes an 'individual,' has no choice but to unite himself with the world in the spontaneity of love and productive work or else to seek a kind of security by such ties with the world as destroy his and the integrity of the individual self.[4]

The closed system is the attractive haven for those who do not want to assume the responsibility of their freedom. The reader should note that the closed system does not use spontaneity of love and productive work, and consequently destroys human potential. Another problem of freedom, besides the responsibility, is that in a democracy there is a virtual state of instability. Biddle, in *The fear of freedom*, notes the 1st Amendment allows critical and disrespectful utterances which tend to create instability.[5] It is this instability that is required for a democracy to function properly. Democracy is a living and developing political form and it grows to the extent that people are free to challenge any and all aspects of the society. The intended outcome is an improved society of advantages for everyone.

The Puritans came to the North American continent to enjoy religious freedom as was mentioned previously. However, religions which are authoritarian, such as the Puritans, do not help people develop their human potential, but rather work to control the adherents. Paul Nash, in *Authority and freedom in education*, points out ". . .authoritarian religions use their strength to enforce censorship and intellectual homogeneity." Nash goes on to say, "Authoritarian religions are antithetical to the development of the intellectual freedom because they assume that they are the holders of absolute truth."[7] The condition which Nash is describing is that of "cults", which are discussed in more detail in chapter seventeen. Cults demonstrate much of the same attitude and behaviors as fanatics. "Religious people express more antihumanitarian attitudes, bigotry, and anxiety than nonbelievers.", according to Nash.[8]

Freedom is not a contradiction which allows people to be kind to their own tribe or group and unkind to others. Freedom is an expression of the complimentary conditions of both freedom and human potential. This is best described by Carl Rogers in *Freedom to learn.*[9] Rogers asserts, "The free person moves out voluntarily, freely, responsibly, to play her significant part in a world whose determined events move through her and through her spontaneous choice and will."[10]

Freedom presents a paradox in that not to have it leaves the person enslaved, but to be free, the person must make the choice and work to achieve it. Freedom is available as a birth-right, but is not acquired passively, it must be actively sought. Freedom is an internal state of being. No form of government or legal system can make a person feel free if that person chooses not to work at removing the ignorance with which they were born. The early years of life, lead many to believe that control is external to them. During this time of development, this is essentially true with one exception. The exception is how you will use your power or energy to explore the world and discover your own freedom. It is much easier for a person to explore and discover when they are in the midst of a culture which is functioning at the highest possible level of integrity. Well integrated people create a cultural environment where people feel safe and will more eagerly explore the world and learn to exercise freedom.

Chapter Sixteen

Paradigm Shift Revisited

Human history is filled with examples of changes of the cultural practices brought about by new awareness of genetic programming and cultural perceptions. Every change has been a shift in emphasis of some of the practices of the culture. These shifts have never been totally complete in that later shifts would not be advantageous or required. The changes often have been resisted, especially by those in positions of authority. This is easier to understand when we look at what Thomas Kuhn said in *The structure of scientific revolutions.*[1] A paradigm shift is preceded by ". . .breakdown and the proliferation of theories. . ."[2] People become less confident in the old paradigm as problems continue to develop and new possibilities of solution are suggested, but ". . .they do not renounce the paradigm that has led them into crisis."[3]

A new paradigm may not be immediately adopted, although it is clearly a more accurate model of what is closer to the truth. Historically, it appears that several things are required before a new paradigm becomes culturally accepted. First of all the crises which are encountered remain essentially unsolved, some alternative approach solves more of the problems than the older beliefs, and a critical mass of people have adopted a new paradigm that solves many of the heretofore unsolved problems. This critical mass is probably not a majority but close to thirty percent of the population. This critical mass becomes influential because most of the remaining seventy percent of the population are at odds and clinging to many ineffectual theories, including the one which led to the crises.

The critical mass has an influence which is unstoppable and the change occurs quickly as one total shift. The gestalt of the new paradigm takes the place of the old gestalt. The new paradigm takes into account the existence of the old paradigm and may incorporate some bits and pieces of it into the new paradigm. The new paradigm reflects an entirely new way of seeing things, a new perception of the matters which led to the problems. It is important to remember the world or reality has not changed. What has changed is how people look at the world, as through new glasses, and they, then approach matters quite differently.

A major obstacle to seeing the new paradigm is the old paradigm has become "the way to see" things in the world. The old paradigm does not facilitate new observations, which have always been possible, and results in them being literally screened out of consciousness. The effect is the same as not being able to see what is plainly visible to the person using the new paradigm. Physiologically nothing registers in the person's awareness of the data that has been, and is still there. Paradigms are powerful and when they shift, interesting things happen.

Joel Barker in a video, *The business of paradigms*, describes how everything changes and what was believed and done before is essentially useless for solving problems. Barker calls this the "going back to zero rule."[4] Everyone who was vested in the old paradigm literally has to go to the start of the new paradigm and begin a new approach to problem solving. This can be observed in many instances in a person's life. Children who leave elementary school for junior high school must start over in this new educational environment. The same is true for junior high students going into high school and high school students going into college. The self-confident person at one stage of education seems to become less mature when then move into the next higher stage. College freshmen look and often act very immature when compared to high school seniors.

A death of a spouse, family member or close friend puts people back to zero. The failure of a business venture or marriage puts people back to zero. Everyone has experienced some paradigm shift in their lives and most people choose to survive and often do quite well. If our ancestors had not survived all the paradigm shifts they encountered, none of us would be here. Paradigms are a natural part of life and they are always changing. Paradigms are the perceptions and beliefs people hold and use to solve their daily problems of living. It seems reasonable then to expect people to change their paradigms when what they are doing is not getting them the results they seek.

Festinger described the effect of cognitive dissonance upon peoples' response to the awareness of a failure in congruency of their beliefs with a new belief they encounter.[5] As presented in chapter eight, these responses run the gamut from not seeing it, through resisting it, and finally to accepting the new belief as possible.[6] Not only are schools filled with unacceptable practices resulting from faulty beliefs or paradigms but anything associated with human endeavor contains paradigms from faulty perceptions. The reader is urged to recall that the natural world really never changes as much as human perceptions about it change. Everything that is going on between and among individuals, groups, classes, and races is the result of the collective paradigms which prevail. When good things are happening, then paradigms of greater positiveness are influencing behaviors and when bad things are happening the paradigms of greater negativeness are the major influences of behavior.

The closed system approach is well entrenched in the activities done in the name of politics. The Greek word *politikos* referred to citizens. From this root comes the modern word politics. As usual the original meaning has been somewhat realigned along lines other than originally intended. What was originally perceived as a necessary practice on behalf of the citizens, has now become something else. Alasdair MacIntyre, a contemporary Virtue Ethicist, in *After virtue* made the observation that by the last quarter of the twentieth century politics had become war by some other means.[7] In the process of completing this draft of this book, I noted a Republican Lobbyist, Tom Korologos' description of the U.S. Senate confirmation hearings of Anthony Lake as Director of the CIA. "Washington is Salem. If we're not lynching somebody 24 hours a day in this wretched town, we're not happy."[8] Anthony Lake subsequently withdrew, with President Clinton's approval a week later. The political pundits attributed the bruising of Mr. Lake to the political back lash from the Democratic National Committee's accepting campaign contributions from disreputable Chinese businessmen. Little was said about Mr. Lakes qualifications for the position.

In my life time the political furor has been constant and seems to be getting more intense. The assassinations of President Kennedy, Rev. Martin Luther King, Jr, and Robert Kennedy are outgrowths of political perceptions held at least by the assassins and probably held by many others. One of my father's brothers, my uncle, told my father that he believed the mess that President Franklin Roosevelt was creating could be solved if all Democrats were lined up and shot. My father's response was, "I'll volunteer to be the first one."

The cultural experience of living, and going to graduate school in Mississippi, provided an opportunity to better understand politics. In 1962-63, I could not tell the ideological difference between Democrats in Mississippi and Republicans in the Dakotas, Nebraska, Wyoming or Iowa and vice versa. It appeared to me that, although the Republican party was formed in the name of liberalism in the mid-nineteenth century to right the conservative tendencies of the Democratic party, that by the mid-twentieth century the two major parties had switched ideologies in the Northern States.

The current President of the U.S. Senate, Trent Lott, of Mississippi, was a Democrat until he decided to run for political office and he switched to the Republican party. This switch was in name only since he was already of the traditionally conservative political party of the Southern States. Senator Lott was just beginning law school at Ole Miss at the time of the forced integration of the University in 1962. This experience may have had a significant effect upon his political development.

The newly formed liberal, Republican party backed its first candidate for president, Abraham Lincoln, and was able to bring about a liberal paradigm shift from the agricultural paradigm of the South to the industrial paradigm of the north. The ending of legalized slavery in the South was a secondary result of this paradigm shift. The period, following the Civil War, known in American History as the Reconstruction Era, was an attempt to bring about the total shift of the paradigm in the South, to which White Southerners were opposed and resisted.

Today the shrewd and suave politician appears to seek the fruits of privilege for himself or herself and his constituency rather than serve and lead the interests of all citizens. In order to do this it becomes at best, game playing or outright war, with the political deaths of the opposition the main focus of the efforts. The notion of liberal versus conservative, in defining social issues, is currently obsolete as the culture moves into the upper part of the curve beyond the point of inflection. Each ideology has attempted to paint its position as being more humane and therefore more patriotic. Since the two major political parties keep moving toward what they believe is the general consensus of the culture, they really reflect more of the perceptions of what those seeking office have, of the public's indications of key social issues. These are not exactly what the public's interests or concerns are. A case in point is the current argument over campaign finance reform, which is what the general population wants but the politicians seem unwilling to address, at this time, through constructive legislation.

A point addressed, in chapter three, about the negative aspects of the closed system and the reliance upon relating to others through weakness, can be revealed by looking at political activities. The U.S. Constitution and Bill of Rights are the two oldest, longest enduring, and most liberal documents in the history of civilizations, which guarantee freedom for the citizens of this democratic form of government. Either ideology runs the risk of misstep when they go to extremes, the far right as conservative and the far left as liberal.

The supporters of the American Revolution were acting on a new liberal paradigm when they challenged the authority of England to control the affairs of the Colonies. In that day, there were those who were opposed to this paradigm shift, away from existing as a plebiscite of England. Today, no one would suggest returning to the pre-Revolutionary relationship with England. In the late 1850's the Democratic party became so rigid in its conservatism that those of a more liberal paradigm created the Republican party. One ideology proclaims patriotism because it holds on to the old paradigm and the other suggests patriotism is in finding a new paradigm to keep alive the search for life, freedom, and pursuit of happiness, unmolested by political interference.

The party which can some how "divine" the will of the people and then package its message, so as to appeal to those whose will is determined, is usually successful in gaining office. The success from that point on, is limited, by the unique design of the U.S. form of democratic government. The balance of power between the executive, legislative, and judicial branches, works to prevent hasty movement in one ideological direction. The closed system approach relies heavily upon attacking the opponent because there must be a "winner and a loser." This stands in sharp contrast to the approach of the open system and that all must be winners.

I have made reference to Hoffer, in the introduction and chapters two and four, where he describes fanaticism as the practice of finding a devil and then working tirelessly to remove it from the face of the earth. This reflects the practices of the closed system where prejudice leads to hate and behind all prejudice is the drive to kill what ever it is that is the embodiment of the negative and false belief. Stephen Holmes in *The anatomy of antiliberalism* says, "Antiliberal writers often jolt their readers awake by identifying a culprit and conducting a trial."[9] Ever since liberal ideas were surfaced in the seventeenth century there have been antagonists which have attacked them. In the United States the improvement of social conditions for all citizens have elements of liberal thought in them. My own mother was one of the first generation of women allowed to vote. This was a powerful paradigm shift for society and women and I seriously doubt if anyone would suggest repealing the 19th Amendment.

Attacking a new paradigm in its earliest stages often reflects the fears of people who perceive dangers for them when everything goes back to zero. Yet it is important for new paradigms to be created to solve the problems the old ones have created. This political arguing is ultimately to the benefit of the evolving paradigm and the people it will effect. The real danger comes from some group trying to control the dialogue so necessary for clarification and transmission of the new paradigm. Following President George Bush's inauguration, the political pundits were surveyed about whether he would exhibit good leadership. George MacGregor Burns said, Bush would be remembered as a leader if he took the American population where they wanted to go.[10] The chairman of the National Conservative Coalition said President Bush would be a good leader to extent he was willing to blame the Democrats for all the problems in society and the world. Blaming takes energy away from problem solving and promotes a worsening of the closed system problems.

The future growth and development of a culture depends upon the creation and transmission of new paradigms to solve old problems. Historically, all of the great political powers, as nations, have survived about two hundred years. The United States is at a dramatic point in the evolution of democracy. Whether the U.S. continues, and to what extent, depends upon the creation of new paradigms. The Roman Catholic Church has survived two thousand years because about every two hundred years it remakes itself through the creation of a new paradigm. There is no need to believe the American culture cannot remake itself. Courage and leadership are required to bring into being a culture with people of the greatest integrity.

Chapter Seventeen

Exemplars of Human Integrity

How will an individual know whether they have integrity? One of the common ways is to find people with considerable integrity and determine if what they display is possible for you. Whether integrity is correctly described as a state of completeness or a point of arrival is uncertain. It appears that integrity is probably always a work in progress. If complete and total integrity is possible, in life as we know it, there are few examples.

The closed system does not promote the development of integrity directly as the open system can. However integrity can be developed from suffering the indignities of the closed system by looking at the dark side of human behavior. For example, I have asked groups and graduate classes to develop lists of those things that would produce dysfunctional youth and adults. This list, unwittingly, describes the common practices of the closed system. Once the practices with which we are familiar are identified in the closed system, then choices of an opposite and positive direction can be made. A simple example I have used, with teachers who rely upon intimidation and humiliation of students as a means of control, is to point out they do not like to be intimidated and humiliated. These teachers are asked how they would rather be related to and they will always say they want to feel safe and accepted. The task then is to internalize this desire for oneself and act on it with respect to everyone. This then reflects a higher degree of integrity.

Christianity, as displayed in the life of Jesus Christ, is an appeal to a higher degree of integrity through always acting out of love. So many examples of the implementation of Christianity are void of this central message of love and acceptance. I worked with a homophobic person who claimed to be a Christian and saw his duty as getting rid of the homosexuals on campus through exclusion, ostracism, intimidation and humiliation. The exemplar of Christianity, Jesus, never advocated this kind of treatment of others nor did he ever display it in his own behavior. This closed system application of Christianity is what places some religious groups in the categories of cults and sects rather than the higher spiritual level that Christ demonstrated.

In my formative years, I was intrigued by the behavior of Mahatma Gandhi as he led India to independence from Great Britain. He was able to achieve a level of integrity, which to this day is rare. He took Thoreau's idea of non-violent civil disobedience and applied it, to a greater extent, in the world, with tremendous success. This was possible because he knew the power of right and good over wrong and bad. It was right to act from the position of conciliation and avoid contention. Had Gandhi acted contentiously he would not have been successful, since he would have only been working to "get the upper hand". His goal was to right the wrong of Colonialism and free the people of India from external exploitation. Gandhi knew that to act contentiously would not remove Colonial practices.

Gandhi was a pioneer in the use of non-violent civil disobedience and had to learn as he led the movement. I was most intrigued by how he used the act of fasting, as a way to move himself to higher awareness and therefore greater integrity. Many interpreted his fasting as exploitation of the masses, who were anxious to get out from under British domination. It has been suggested that the masses were so afraid he would die from fasting that they would stop rioting just to save Gandhi's life. This may have been a part of it as far as the masses were concerned. Gandhi never wanted to scare anyone or leave anyone without a leader, his mission was simply to restore the sovereignty of India and secure freedom for the citizens of India.[1] The assassination of Gandhi ended his life but not the movement he led.

Martin Luther King, Jr. took up the tool of non-violent civil disobedience in the 1960's during the Civil Rights movement in the United States. It seemed clear to me that King knew what Gandhi had learned and demonstrated. How much integrity Dr. King had is still debated, but I believe he had more integrity than those who hated him and were responsible for his assassination. He also worked for conciliation and not from the position of contentiousness. What he wanted was equality for all American citizens regardless of race, creed, or skin color. His leadership contributed significantly to the improvement of equality and is still an inspiration to many.

Abraham Maslow was looking for reasons as to why some people achieve higher levels of functioning when he conceived the idea of the self-actualizing person. He divided all human needs into to broad categories, the basic group he called deficiency needs and the higher group he called growth needs. To become self-actualizing implies that all needs lower in the hierarchy must be met. Much of what goes on in the closed system works against everyone having access to the basic or deficiency needs. Poverty is created in the closed system from beliefs such as win/lose and scarcity which are aggravated by prejudice. Integrity, as a power base for living, never gets well developed in the closed system because the limited energy of the person is spent on just staying alive. A Black mother, an inhabitant of a ghetto, was approached by school officials and admonished that if she really cared about her children, she would see to it that they were in school everyday. Through tear filled eyes she said, "I do care about my children, I spend all of my energy trying to keep a roof over their heads and food on the table. I don't have any more energy to give."

Maslow's *Motivation and personality* contains the

names of historical and public figures he was fairly sure were self-actualized.[2] His list contains the names of Jefferson, Lincoln, William James, Jane Addams, Spinoza, Eleanor Roosevelt, Aldous Huxley, and Einstein. These judgments reflect his impressions based upon his theory of self-actualization.

Erick Erickson's model of human development, which came to my attention weeks after leaving Mississippi in 1963, has provided a framework or paradigm for me to consider the whole issue of integrity. Erickson conceptualized the development of humans as occurring as the result of learning eight different life skills in a natural sequence.[3] Later, Gail Sheehy in *Passages* indicated that not only are the life skills necessary but if they are not learned at the appropriate developmental stage the person will experience a difficult passage into the next stage.[4]

My particular experiences as a junior high school teacher suggested the fifth stage was of paramount importance to me. The fifth stage of identity was so significant, especially for eighth grade students.[5] Larry, the boy mentioned in the introduction, who had lost his father and grandfather was questioning his own identity. It was at this point that teaching science became secondary to my being there for youths, who were working on their identities. Youth who leave this age period, at about fifteen years of age, with a failure identity are usually lost to themselves and society. To make winners and losers for life is the agenda of the closed system and those in schools often, unknowingly contribute to the loss of human potential. My desire was then to make every effort to assure that each youth, with whom I had contact, would leave this age period with a sense of success.

The first stage of Erickson's model is the development of trust during the first year of life. Without this life skill, all other stages will be problematic. Trust of others is built upon trust of oneself. When adults do not respond in safe, nurturing, and predictable ways, an infant does not learn to trust and is emotionally crippled until this skill is learned.

The term mid-life crisis is a descriptor of much of what is experienced when a "passage" to next stage begins. Sheehy observes that in mid-life many people respond to the crisis in life by changing careers, changing mates, or getting another degree.[6] None of these actions, in and of themselves, is an adequate remediation of the lack of development in some earlier stage.

Gwen Hawley produced an instrument for measuring the extent of development in each of Erickson's eight stages called the *Measures of Psychosocial Development (MPD)*.[7] Graduate students, in leadership development classes, report a high reliability of measure of what they intuitively already suspect about themselves. The self selection of people enrolling in this kind of assessment driven experience, thus far, has not included anyone who is seriously neurotic or psychotic.

One male student's profile showed considerable conflict at the trust stage. In discussion with him about the results, he revealed that he had been severely abused by his father while a child at home. At the time of our discussion, he was estranged from his father. The most notable observation of this young man was, that although he was very intellectually bright he was constantly on guard against any impropriety directed toward him. If he suspected any violation of law, rules of fairness, or moral lapse he would retaliate with great precision in his attack on the "wrong doer." He knew the rules and regulations better than anyone and in effect used them as a club. He has had a troubled employment record and finds it difficult to secure any position which would require significant leadership for which he holds credentials. His hostility toward authority is revealed, sometimes subtly, during the interview process and is easily detected as the lack of trust it is. This lack of trust is evidence of a lack of integrity.

Integrity is the eighth and last stage of Erickson's model. This is the stage when people are able to achieve a level of self-satisfaction about their lives and accomplishments. In chapter one, reference was made to Thoreau's observation that "the mass of men live quiet lives of desperation. . ."[8] Despair is the result of a lack of integrity and comes from a realization of lost opportunities and a lack of time to undo them.

Stephen Carter's book *Integrity* contains this definition:

> . . .integrity, applied to a person, carries more than a sense of wholeness, because a person must have something to be whole about. It carries more than a sense of perfection, because the person must have a standard against which that perfection is measured. And the thing that the person of integrity is whole about, the standard against which perfection is measured, is "uncorrupted virtue' and a sense of 'uprightness, honesty, [and] sincerity."[9]

The internal quotation marks represent Carter's acknowledgment of the pieces of the definition as found in the Oxford English Dictionary. This definition brings us back to the importance of knowing oneself as discussed in chapter one. The thing that "a person of integrity is whole about" is how fully he or she has achieved his or her potential as a functioning human being. This wholeness is difficult to measure when what it means to be a human is not clear.

Wholeness does not exist independently of some standard as noted in Carter's definition. This wholeness must be in relation to "something." I believe this "something" has everything to do with a person's moral development as described in chapter 13 and displayed in Figure 13.1. It is very possible that a person can be very intelligent, in the intellectual sense, but not well developed morally, spiritually, physically, or emotionally. This kind of person is not whole compared to the standard of integrity.

INTEGRITY, COURAGE, & SOUL 221

Figure 17.1
ORIENTATIONS TO RELATIONSHIPS

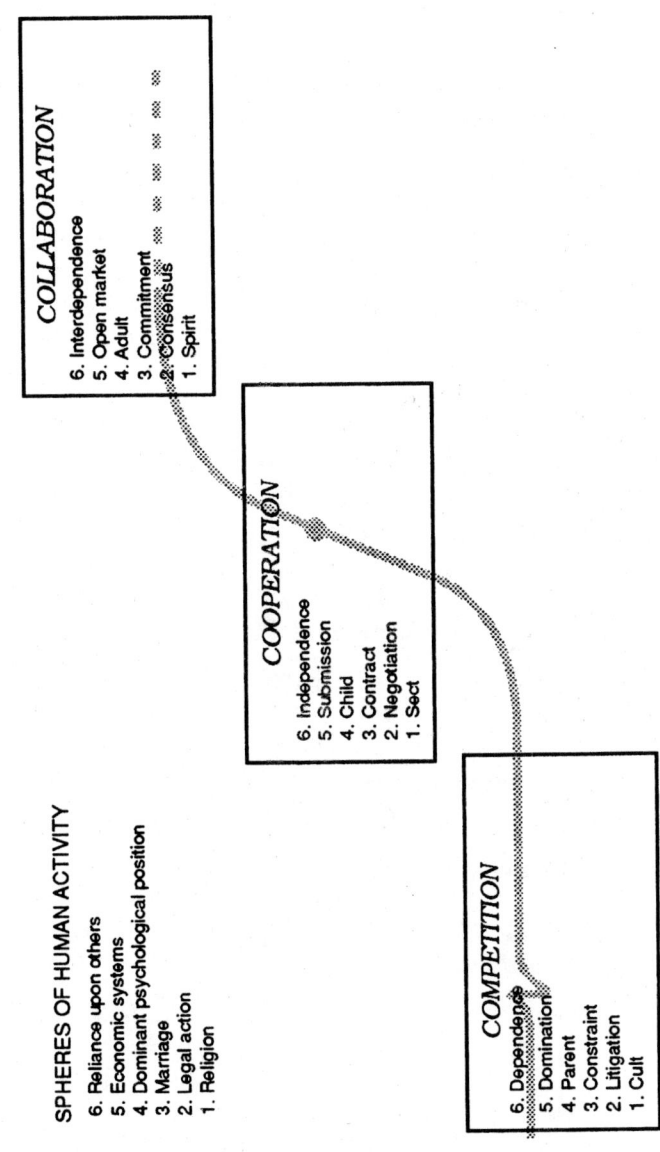

Figure 17.1 displays the levels of development for orientations to relationships, superimposed upon the sigmoid curve. People are born into the world as nomads, but quickly are subjected to the closed system and are acculturated to be closed to themselves, others, and the world. This type of acculturation is not necessary, but represents the best our ancestors were able to do, given their cultural experiences. It has become abundantly clear that humans can move well beyond the biological commands of their genes and develop cultural orientations which convey standards of behavior known as memes. The problems in a culture are more debilitating to the individuals when the culture gets stuck in antiquated cultural prescriptions and hence results in a dysfunctional culture.

The American culture reflects many preferences for the practices listed in the lower end of the sigmoid curve in figure 17.1 and therefore is the embodiment of the closed system. Six relationship situations, or spheres of human activity, are numbered in each of the boxes on the sigmoid curve. These six relationships or spheres of human activity are: 1. religion, 2. legal action, 3. marriage, 4. dominate psychological position, 5. economics, and 6. reliance upon others.

The first stage is named *COMPETITION*. The six elements listed above are given names specific to competition. Cults are in competition with all other beliefs, so use practices which isolate the followers from their families, other beliefs and society in general. In earlier times, a cult group would move to an isolated or remote part of the country or world to more fully indoctrinate the followers. Today it is possible for a cult, such as Heaven's Gate, to live in an expensive suburb of San Diego and still be isolated from society.

The legal system relies upon litigation or court action to win. And the person who is being hauled into court is the loser and must pay with either, money and time or his or her life. A successful lawyer is one who always wins, whether the person they represent is guilty of the crime with which they are charged. Finding the prosecution guilty of some violation which stops the court action is a win. The prosecution then loses.

Item number 3 is a reflection of the earliest orientations of a man "taking" a wife. When a man would find a woman he wanted, he simply took her from her family. The characterization of a man in leopard skin dragging a woman into his cave by the hair is not far from the original reality. Some have surmised that the role of the "best man" came about during these times as an aide in the abduction of the woman.

The next term, parent, comes from the body of psychology known as Transactional Analysis (TA). The parent can either be nurturing or punishing. In the closed system the parent is more punishing. Children and youth require nurturing, but in the closed system they get punishment in the name of discipline.

A significant piece of human relationships is bound up in economics. The goal of economics, at this lower end of the sigmoid curve, is domination. As a matter of fact, greatness is attributed to "market domination" more so than to being of service to people. Market domination relies upon many practices which reflect the three lowest levels of the moral development sequence. Some businesses rely upon going to court, and winning big, to gain advantage in the market place.

The sixth and remaining item at the lower end of the sigmoid curve is dependence. Every effort is made to assure that all others are dependent upon those in authority. The exploitation of others, making them losers, is necessary to maintain this position. There would be no dependence if there were no losers. As one parent asked me, in arguing publicly for ability groups, in junior high English classes, "How will we know our children are doing well if they are not in the advanced level classes?" In response, I said something like, "Let me see if I understand. If your neighbor's child is in the low ability group and your child is in the high ability group, you will know your child is doing well. In other words if your neighbor's child is losing out then yours is doing well." I think this sums up the agenda of competition. It is war where someone is defeated and someone wins. This is immoral, to deliberately destroy others so those with influence can call themselves winners. The winners always blame the losers for being weak and less fit or deserving of privilege.

The most highly researched and reported account of competition is Alfie Kohn's *No contest: the case against competition.*[10] Kohn says that we are trained to compete and believe in competition.[11] This training is built upon three myths; 1. it is human nature, 2. it is motivating for one to do better, and 3. it builds character.[12] My experiences with early adolescents, in junior high schools, very clearly revealed to me the negative affect, of competition, upon these young people. They do not want to compete with their friends since it destroys the relationship. One class of eighth grade science students demonstrated this through a form of mutiny. They would not work for grades given on a curve. It wasn't until I worked out a grading system which reflected each one's best effort against past efforts that they began to enjoy and work in science class.

The deep rootedness of competition is reflected in the pleadings of politicians. They have been demanding better schools since 1983, and the release of *The Nation at Risk,*[13] "so that America can regain the competitive edge in the world." Also, President Johnson declared war on poverty, there have been wars declared on illiteracy, President Reagan appointed a "Drug Czar" to head the war on drugs, and now we have a whole new effort directed toward volunteerism to help youth. The living ex-presidents were asked to endorse this effort and President Ford said, "We will win this war." The introduction of competition into relationships ". . .actually make us less successful."[14] Kohn suggests there is not one arena of human relationships that could not be improved by moving to cooperativeness.[15]

Cooperativeness is an improvement, but it is not where the human is capable of moving. Where competitiveness is driven by the dictum, "What's mine is mine and what's yours is mine, if I can get it away from you.", cooperativeness lives by, "What I have, I'll share, if you have something to share in return." Cooperation lessens the blow of being a loser, since the valuables of the haves are shared. The losers are still losers and they know it, because as soon as they have nothing to share, they do not get anything. This is the reason why I have displayed cooperation within the closed system. The unequal advantage still remains and can trigger the fears of both. Because of a lack of integrity, or not knowing what to do with fear, people will return to the lower end of the sigmoid curve, to engage in war.

What originally began as "cooperative learning" in schools was indeed cooperative, and not very successful for very long. Children and youth trained in the closed system always believe in winning and losing. Very bright youth, grouped with the less capable students, get very upset at having to share so much and get so little in return. Parents of very bright students do not want their children to share with the less capable student because, "Their children will be held back by doing this."

Returning to figure 17.1, examination of the *COOPERATION* section on the sigmoid curve shows sect as the religious orientation. A sect is often thought of as splinter group from some other longer established group. These people have found the cult orientation to be too confining and they are seeking more individual freedom but still see the need for compliance of the followers. They follow very clear sets of rules for worship but do not expect the degree of blind obedience required by the cult.

The legal orientation moves away from court action or litigation into negotiation. The idea is to bring about, "give and take," without getting into the open combativeness of war. In 1964, I became extensively involved in the negotiations on behalf of a local teachers organization. I was one of seven teachers who negotiated directly with the seven member school board. After some initial war-like skirmishes, we finally got down to negotiating. As members of the local teachers organization, we presented a list of items to be negotiated. After much give and take on these items, I was satisfied there had been new potential for improvement in the working conditions. When it came time to vote, as negotiators, on acceptance of the agreement achieved, three of our committee said, "Let's not accept any of them and vote to go on strike." I was shocked at this suggestion and asked, "Why strike?" The general response of the dissenters was, "They have made us hurt, so we need to make them hurt?" The attitude of cooperativeness prevailed and no strike occurred. This shows how easy it is to slip back into the war like mentality of win and lose. The thinking was, that cooperating was not making the school board look enough like losers, like the teachers believed they had been.

A new contract was signed as a result of this negotiation and working conditions improved which contributed to improved instruction of children. To continue to follow the format of figure 17-1, the word contract is a continuation of the relationship efforts in marriage. Women were no longer to be over powered by a man that wanted to possess them, but some effort was made to allow some negotiation. In cults, no negotiation is allowed, many young girls are just assigned to the man by the family. If there is negotiation, it is between the girl's family and the prospective husband or owner. Some families provide large dowries as enticements for a man to take this girl off their hands. The marriage vows are a contract, but you can go back to the lower end of the sigmoid curve and litigate the contract and get a divorce or nullify the contract.

All of the psychological underpinnings of this intermediate step are at developing a child like relationship. The person is to be obedient, conforming, and happy. The age of games keeps the child occupied and out of trouble since these games all require stringent adherence to well defined rules. The child can be either happy or wounded. The very nature of the closed system always wounds the child. The basic wound is a lack of proper development of integrity which produces the pain of the soul.

In order for a person to survive in the closed system at the level of cooperation, they must submit to the parental authority of the lower end of the sigmoid curve. The child's very existence is tied to domination by the parental psychological orientation. The person, held in this state of dormancy, never goes on to develop into a fully functioning human. The only choices they see are to remain submissive or to become like those who dominate them. This is the basic cultural situation which Freire described as the oppressed becoming the oppressors.[16]

Submission has become a tool of a patriarchal economic system in that the general public is to submit to the enticements which comes from Madison Avenue. The consumer public is expected to buy what is produced for their consumption, and all sorts of tactics are employed. The ultimate end is always the same, submit to the ploys of advertising and buy the products to boost the profits of the corporation. The example of a tactic, is the approach taken, after the 19th amendment was adopted, to get women to smoke more cigarettes. The American Tobacco Company enlisted the expertise of Sigmond Freud's nephew, Edward L. Bernays. Mr. Bernays used what he called *engineered consent* to co-opt the taboo of women smoking in public. He suggested that a group of debutantes march in the Easter Parade in New York City smoking cigarettes. They were invited to do this using the enticement of, "Ladies, light up your torches of freedom!" These attractive women were photographed and made the front page of the New York Times. The rest is history. The taboo was gone with that one news release. Women were kept in the closed system to be exploited by the tobacco companies in the name of increased freedom.

The final stage of cooperation, independence, is a myth. Independence is not possible in the closed system. The person who believes he or she is independent always relies on something or somebody of which to be independent. Yet in the closed system this is presented as a goal of the middle segment of the sigmoid curve. It is a misguided notion, which at best, gives people a goal to work toward. The problem is that when working on this goal, the person is not likely to see the next stage of development, that of collaboration.

The open system, or upper stage, of the sigmoid curve is the stage of *COLLABORATION* in human relationships. Arrival at this stage of relationship is through hard work against many threats and invitations to remain in the closed system. To remain at this level is also hard work. There never has been a cultural majority living at this level and many of those who did live at his level have been killed or silenced. Living at this level puts a person in a very vulnerable position in the culture. It almost seems a paradox that a person must be vulnerable to live effectively. Yet this is exactly the case, to be alive in the present moment is to be vulnerable. A person of high integrity, because of being alive in the present moment, can actually be more effective at life and therefore the desired role model for the younger generation.

The open system requires skills in relationships which include being spiritual or loving. The ability to accept all humans, unconditionally, as gifts of creation, puts the person in a position of being able to collaborate with others. Where competition is based on getting everything a person can, and cooperation is a conditional sharing, collaboration is giving away what one has to those who need it. The Native American people regularly give away what they have. It is a remarkable experience to be invited to a "Give Away" and be given a gift. Our gift was a star quilt. Someday we will have to give it away to someone. Giving what you have to others is the fullest act of compassion, especially when the gift is love, the unconditional regard for humans.

In the open system, consensus is the desired goal, rather than the war like maneuverings of litigation or game like playing of negotiations. In consensus everyone agrees on the circumstances or actions to be taken. It is a mutual agreement among equals rather some forced or contrived trick to outwit another. Everyone is a winner with no losers.

In the case of marriage, the open system is looking for a commitment, which is what marriage vows contain.

The taking of someone to be a lawfully wedded spouse, for richer or poorer, in sickness and health, for the good times and the bad times, until death do they part, is a suggestion of a needed commitment. It is my observation that marriages fail because one or both did not take the invitation to commitment to heart. As soon as another person looks more sexually alluring, the person splits or if rough times come along they split. All of the things that confront a marriage relationship are all gifts, or invitations to continue one's growth to greater integrity. The ability to not yield to temptations and to stay committed in hard times are strengths which are possible through increased integrity.

TA describes adult directed living as the desired position, which puts the control in the rational part of the person's ego. A strong adult component of the personality is the regulator which allows the nurturing parent to nurture and not punish and the happy child to grow and play, and not become wounded or act out of the woundedness.

The economics of the open system is best described by Henderson as a win/win system.[18] She describes a four part economic system instead of the typical two part system of public and private. Henderson uses the model of a three layer cake with icing as the basic structure. The first layer is the natural world and therefore includes people and children as the basic raw material to be developed. The second layer is volunteerism which accounts for a great amount of the economy but is never factored in when figuring economic productivity and efficiency.

The traditional economic model, of public and private, gives very little credence to either the natural world or volunteerism as being economically important. However they represent the very foundation upon which both the public and private sectors rest. The public sector or third layer of cake, contains only those aspects of human need which cannot generate a profit. And the private sector or the icing between the layers and covering the cake, is that part of the economy which generates wealth and profit, which in turn must continually be reinvested in the cake. The private sector or icing cannot effectively function without the three layers of cake below in good functioning order. Kozol describes what happens when the private sector decides not to provide for the development of children in his book *Savage inequalities.*[19] The entire culture is impacted when the private sector does not put back into the system to replace what is used up and repair what has been damaged in the environment.

American economists have extolled the virtues of "free enterprise." There is no free enterprise left in the public, legitimate market. The only place free enterprise is alive and well is in the illicit drug trade, sex related trade of prostitution and pornography, and flea markets or garage sales. The first two are labeled as illegal, but because they are truly free enterprise they are very difficult to shut down. Neither of these would be attractive to anyone if the culture was truly open and a win/win situation.

The sixth and remaining item in the collaboration level of relationships is recognition that all humans need something from all other humans. The recognition of interdependence in the open system helps not only those seeking basic development but those who have achieved high levels of development. Not only are children and youth in need of adult assistance, adults need to help the youth. We are all interdependent with everyone else. What one person does affects all others; when it is positive, everyone benefits. The open system promotes the highest integrity which can be accurately described .

Returning to Carter's definition of integrity, it is clear that some people have managed, against forces, to the contrary, to discover both aspects of integrity. They have discerned what it is to be a fully functioning human and how they measure up to this standard. It is these people I suggest we call exemplars of integrity. The purpose of this book is to identify these traits and skills possible through integrity as something to be learned by everyone in a free society.

I believe we already know more than enough to educate the youth to greater levels of integrity and therefore are not exhibiting integrity by not doing so. To know how to prevent the closed system from destroying the hopes of achieving integrity and allow the closed system to prevail is first of all unwise and secondly it is immoral. When the five domains of energy or power; intellectual, moral, physical, emotional and spiritual, are not fully developed and interconnected, there is a lack of integrity, courage, and soul.

Chapter Eighteen

The Future of Integrity in the Face of Chaos

Chaos is the term used by people who cannot see order in what they are experiencing or observing. As stated in chapter four, there is no chaos in the natural world. There may be calamity such as a floods, volcanic eruptions, and earthquakes. The reason for the losses, felt by humans, is from ignorance of the impending natural forces with which they have placed themselves in close proximity. Famine and poverty are the collective result of the prevailing belief systems of people. The belief that there is never going to be enough material wealth for everyone is still anchored in Malthus' pronouncement that population expands exponentially and wealth expands arithmetically.[1] To believe this, is to not see the open system paradigm, but only the closed system paradigm, which is all that Malthus saw. There is ample evidence to indicate that disease is really "dis-ease" and therefore is under the control of the people in many cases. To believe chaos is a part of the natural world is pessimistic and negative.

The future comforts and successes of the culture depend upon integrity. Therefore integrity has a very bright future in the face of imagined disorder. As people develop more integrity they will act more courageously because they will be drawing on the power of the soul. This does not mean that people will not experience pain and discomfort. Pain, both physical and spiritual, is a gift of creation the same as shame and fear. Had our ancestors not listened to these, we would not be here.

Integrity gives a person the tools to recognize the gifts of pain, shame, and fear and to use them to correct their thoughts and actions. The male model has insisted that men don't feel pain, shame, and fear to the detriment of men and the culture. Could it be true, as some suggest, that women have a higher tolerance for pain? I would not rule out the ability of women to be able to more effectively deal with pain, because they have been allowed to own it. Being able to openly feel pain has given women an opportunity to learn how to handle it. No one can learn how to handle anything if they don't openly acknowledge its presence. Pain is part of a gift which is to be welcomed as it informs one of impending calamity.

Integrity means the ability to welcome pain and joy as both necessary and useful in a person's evolution to higher levels of functioning. Language from chemistry captures the essence of these two feelings. Pain and joy are isomers in that they contain the same numbers of the same elements but in different configurations and with different properties. To have integrity is to hold pain and joy in tautomeric balance. Pain becomes joy and joy becomes pain as they are held in equilibrium. They can readily change into the other when each is accepted and it is understood that each is the "raw material" for the other.

When a person does not accept the necessity of pain they exclude it as long as possible, all the while seeking to increase their joy. Not accepting pain leaves the person with no "raw material" out of which to produce joy. This lack of joy eventually gives way to tremendous pain. It is as though the pain is saying, "I am here, use me to build the joy you seek." The most remarkable recoveries from some painful disaster are described by people as receiving a gift and they are now much stronger. The gift of pain is there all along and they were forced into accepting it, and building from it. They are stronger in integrity. Sometimes it seems to me that in spite of our ignorances, which we often refuse to admit, we are still led to the inherent possibilities of becoming fully human whether we know it or not. Some of us would rather believe in chaos and therefore we have no influence over what is going wrong. Chaos is nothing more than a faulty description of something we have not yet learned.

What is lacking to a great extent in our culture are those who can model the aspect of integrity which helps us navigate the choppy waters of too much pain or joy. Virtue ethics describes the mean between two extremes. We cannot be virtuous if we do not recognize and accept the vices on either side. Too much food is gluttony and too little food is starvation while integrity calls for eating plenty of the nutritious foods, but not to the point of excess. Not only should one not eat more than is required for body functioning, but should recognize that some fat storage may be required in a time of food shortage. The same is true for joy. One should welcome joy but not at the exclusion of the real possibility of pain. Real joy comes from knowing that pain is inevitable at some time but it brings with it the material out of which new joy can be built.

Joy is often experienced in the form of what Maslow called peak experiences.[2] William James called them mystic experiences.[3] The mystic or peak experience is a loss of self or transcendence and intense enjoyment. Mihaly Csikszentmihaly describes this condition as the opposite of psychic entropy and calls the optimal experience *flow*.[4] These seem to be fairly common experiences and others can detect when someone is in this type of experience. I have had situations in which I either had or came very close to flow or peak experiences. The first incident was when playing in a high school basketball game, I scored 21 points in the first half where normally I would have only scored four or five points. I experienced this as a moment of complete harmony within me, everything I did was right and I never had felt better. Forty years later when I met Coach Oorlog at a reunion, the first words out of his mouth were, "Do you remember the night you scored 21 points in the first half, against Hill City?"

While I was working, on campus, to complete the doctoral degree at Arizona State University, about twenty years later, I had another experience while running during lunch time. After the usual weightlifting and calisthenics, I would run two or three miles on the outdoor track. I first became aware that running was not a struggle and that I seemed to be floating with the greatest of ease. I didn't know my running was being watched by others. Not only did my running mate, Fred Mills, come over to me and ask me what had happened but people I never met before came and asked me what I had done to run like that. Again this felt like complete harmony and ease of effort, yet accomplishing something in a way never possible in the regular experience.

The most discomfiting thing for me, in both cases, was not being able to directly re-induce these states of enjoyment at will. They seemed to have come from somewhere and then went back to wherever they came. The closest thing to having repeated experiences have come through my teaching experiences at the college level. There have been many times when I felt like a spectator, watching myself lead a class through a challenging and new paradigm. Much of what I have written in this book comes out of those experiences. I often told students I would hate to miss one of my classes since so many new insights were always being brought forth. Teaching others what is contained in this book has provided me with the closest thing to mystical and flow or peak experiences.

The things which lead us to more clarity and out of our ignorance are to be found in the open system. If we become closed by our experiences in the closed system, we may never recognize the closed system perceptions and the end result is misery and confusion. The sense of helplessness we feel from our misery and confusion, can be an invitation to open ourselves to the greater possibilities, even when we cannot see them. This openness to new paradigms will take us beyond our current perceptions, which are largely rooted in the closed system. Our perceptions, when left unexamined, can hold us hostage, and our **un**willingness to explore new perceptions, puts us fully in charge of our own misery.

My experiences in public education have provided an important insight into what is partially the cause of what people are calling the "failure" of public education. First of all public education has not been a failure. America's system of public education is the envy of the world and has been copied by many countries. American public education has been a phenomenal success and done largely what Jefferson had imagined it would. We would not be a thriving democracy, had schools not been successful. However, for public education to continue in the form in which it was created is wrong.

In 1983, *The nation at risk* was released with dire predictions for the future of American Society.[5] Close examination of the document suggests the recommended solutions are to be found in basically continuing to do the same things, for more days out of the year, with longer days, and higher standards. The results have not been what some policy makers imagined. Yet it is very clear, that if what you are doing is wrong, you will only get more of the same in greater quantity and in shorter periods of time. We need to remember Einstein's insight, "We can't solve problems by using the same kind of thinking we used when we created it."[6] The public school system was created in the closed system, built on the practices of prejudice, punishment, and praise. It has served the needs of a developing society, but now must move on to less cruel and inhumane educational practices.

The common practices of making schools more effective, that is increased student learning, can be organized under seven different categories. These are new curricula, textbooks, replacement of incompetent staff, reorganization, remodeling or new construction of facilities, libraries, and instructional gadgetry. These things are all necessary and desirable, yet they are not resulting in increased student learning. When you listen to the students, they tell you what they want; teachers who care about them as human beings. The closed system does not contribute much to caring about children in ways in which they feel safe and therefore willing to take the risks involved in being open to new possibilities. American public education requires a new paradigm shift to teaching children and youth in ways which will recognize them as gifts-not burdens and as the most important asset any culture has. The answer to the paradigm shift question for education is, "Every child learning in every class, everyday, all year long." Thinking about this, as a new paradigm, will lead to the changes which make it happen. There will be much turmoil (chaos) because many are so vested in the closed system model of education they will resist the new opportunities.

The entire culture will benefit from a new educational paradigm built on the belief that it is wrong to deliberately create misery for others and allow existing miseries to continue unabated. The open system of education will rest upon the integrity of the second generation of educators who have the integrity and therefore the courage to move beyond those desires to perpetuate the closed system.[7] Teachers with soul will act out of love, discipline, and encouragement. The youth will have stronger souls and not be drawn to addictive practices as a means to escape the pain and misery with which they are currently living. This stronger intervention in the lives of youth, from the efforts of educators, will lead to stronger parenting. Parents are rightfully proud and feel more capable when their children do well in school. Parents whose children do poorly in school feel helpless and without recourse.

Not only are children society's greatest natural resource, but teachers are a very valuable cultural asset. No other society, than the United States of America, has as many highly qualified educators, per capita, as the United States. Some teachers struggle with my suggestion that it is the teacher's responsibility to change children from losers into winners. This, they say is impossible. I ask them for the alternative. Many conclude that the only alternative is to make sure every child learns not only the formal curriculum but how to live positively.

I believe the future of the American society depends upon the success of public education to educate a new generation of educators who can produce a generation of open system citizens. This will be more easily accomplished if the history of cultural evolution is taught and learned. The American dream has come true for some but not for everyone. The work of the first decade of the new millennium will be to create a society where everyone can gain the needed advantages for a productive and fulfilling life.

People are born as nomads and therefore must traverse the likes of the sigmoid curve and all that it implies. It is my intention that this book will shorten the time people spend wandering, as nomads, in the "garden" of great possibilities. I believe it is necessary for each person to be guided through the historical evolution of culture, lest they become infatuated with and settle for an imperfect intermediate step.

I am reminded of a quote from Ernst Heinrich Haeckel, often repeated to students in biology classes. The following is from *The history of creation.*

> Ontogenesis, or the development of the individual, is a short and quick recapitulation of the phylogenesis, or the development of the tribe to which it belongs, determined by the laws of inheritance and adaptation.[8]

This statement, I believe, suggests that just as an individual retraces the biological (genes) of the species during the embryonic stage, the individual retraces the cultural history (memes) of the culture during his or her life time. The development of the individual is determined by both genes and memes - inheritance and adaptation. The culture, being made up of individuals, needs a critical mass of individuals to move cultural evolution to the next level of development of the human species. Humans have not yet arrived in the open system in adequate enough numbers to provide a significant example of an open society. How long this will take is not certain, but my hope is for it to happen in my life time and that of my children and grand children.

EPILOGUE

A commonly heard moral story, *The Three Little Pigs*, offers some insights into the essence of the overall message of this book.[1] After writing the initial draft, I became aware of some connections with this gruesome tale and the concept of integrity, as I have described and defined it. The oldest versions of this tale are more gruesome than the later versions. These later versions possibly are intended to protect the innocence of the children who hear them. Yet it is the original rendition which seems more appropriate. Some part of the message is lost, besides the words, in the softening of this tale. I believe the originators intended a deeper meaning available through intuitive insight. I believe this story conveys an understanding of what it takes to make it in the cruel world, essentially integrity, courage, and soul.

The story describes a mother pig who has determined it is time to send her three little pigs out into the world to make it on their own. This is a typical family situation, especially when the parents have given their children everything they can give them in the way of moral upbringing. Each child must make it into the world on his own, the parents have done all they can.

The first little pig encounters a man with a bundle of straw and asks to have the straw to build himself a house. The mother pig has warned them all not to be taken in by anything but to always seek the most desirable. Apparently this little pig does not recognize that straw is not very strong but it does provide considerable comfort as a place to live. Straw symbolizes the easy availability of what is offered in the first level of the closed system. There is plenty of straw around and it can make a person comfortable up to a point. It is easy to see why the first little pig got what he asked for so easily.

However the wolf comes by and warns the little pig that he will huff and puff and blow his house down. The little pig felt perfectly safe in this house of his own construction, so took no precautions. And, so the wolf huffs and puffs and blows his straw house down and eats the pig. Since this is a moral story, it seems as though the wolf is intended to symbolize the sinister aspects of living in the first or lowest stage of the closed system. Although there are warnings of the closed system being unsafe, the pig is unable to recognize them and feels confident what he has found, was what his mother advised him to seek. It is easy to see how one can ignore the warnings and wind up in the wolfs belly and everything that implies.

The second little pig sets out and encounters a man with a bundle of sticks and asks for the bundle of sticks so he can build his house. The sticks are readily given to him and he builds a very comfortable house. The wolf comes by and warns him that he will huff and puff and blow his house down. The second little pig is sure he did not commit the same error as his brother and so he takes no precautions. And so the wolf huffs and puffs and blows the stick house down and eats the second little pig.

The moral of the story continues which reveals there is more than one way to be deceived in the closed system. The sinister aspect is active in more than one arena and so therefore finds weakness in the second stage of the closed system, although those living there seem oblivious to the dangers, even after being warned by the wolf. So too, the second little pig is devoured by the closed system.

Now the third little pig has obviously learned from the mistakes of his two siblings. He encounters a man with a load of bricks and asks for them to build a house. The bricks are readily given and he builds a comfortable home. In due time, since the wolf knows there are three pigs, the wolf comes along and warns the third little pig of his intent to huff and puff and blow his house down. The third little pig is confident his house will stand, so is not too concerned, but continues with the preparation of a boiling cauldron of water in the fireplace.

The wolf huffs and puffs and puffs and huffs and is finally exhausted. Not so exhausted that he is unable to climb to the roof of the brick house. The wolf is intent upon getting this little pig and in desperation, drops down the chimney into the boiling pot of water. After the wolf is overcome with the extreme experience of being boiled alive, the third little pig pulls him out of the pot and cuts open his belly. Out jump the first and second little pigs and they have a joyous meal together and live happily ever after.

The brick house symbolizes the third stage of the sigmoid curve which is in the open system. The bricks symbolize all of the lessons of life which are learned through much toil and pain. Each brick is a symbol of the integration of the elements of the closed system; the straw, sticks, and earth or clay. When these elements are taken without modification and with little integration, they are weak. Burning the straw and sticks to heat the clay makes a durable brick. The closed system contains all of the material and energy for constructing an integrated life in the open system, where one can feel safe and secure, and then help those who are stuck in the belly of the wolf or the closed system.

It is my hope through acceptance of the closed system, as a source of raw materials, and through the active process of love, we can all escape the belly of the wolf and can build a more joyful and successful life in the open system for ever and ever.

END NOTES

Introduction

[1] Kant, Immanuel, 1956. *Groundwork of the metaphysic of morals,* Translated and analysed by H. J. Paton. New York: Harper Torchbooks/The Academy Library.

[2] Postman, Neil and Charles Weingartner, 1969. *Teaching as a subversive activity.* New York: Delacorte Press.

[3] Freire, Paulo, 1970. *Pedagogy of the oppressed.* New York: Herder and Herder.

[4] Hutchins, Robert M., 1953. *The conflict in education in a democratic society.* New York: Harper and Row Publishers. Reprinted in 1972 by Greenwood Press.

[5] Strand, Ray D. MD. In the spring or late winter of 1983, Dr. Strand spoke to an adult group on the spiritual connection to healing and holistic medicine generally. This meeting was held at Westminster Presbyterian Church in Rapid City, South Dakota.

Chapter One

[1] Thoreau, Henry David, September 7, 1851. This statement was written in his personal journal. This citation comes from *Bartlet's Familiar Quotations,* Fifteenth and 125th Anniversary Edition, 1982. Boston: Little, Brown and Company.

[2] Thoreau, Henry David, 1854. *Walden.* This citation is taken from *The great books,* Chicago: The Great Books Foundation. First Year, Volume 8, Number 15. p. 33.

[3] Reisman, David, 1961. *The lonely crowd: a study of the changing American character.* New Haven: Yale University Press. p. 15.

[6] McCrone, John, 1991. *The ape that spoke: language and the evolution of the human mind.* New York: William Morrow and Company, Inc. p. 26.

[5] Einsten, Albert. 1879-1955. This statement is attributed to Einstein. The Institute for Advanced Study, in Princeton, New Jersey, where Einstein taught, is unable to find when he said this, in what publication it is recorded, and the context in which he said it. The only source of the quote they found was at a web site at Stanford University on Einstein's quotes. This source provided no background on the quote.

⁶Plato. References are to the prescriptions for society taken from the *Republic* contained in the paperback book, *The great dialogues of Plato*. Translation by W. H. D. Rouse, 1956. New York: Mentor Books.

Chapter Two

¹Campbell, Joseph, 1988. *The power of myth: with Bill Moyers*. Edited by Betty Sue Flowers. New York: Doubleday. p. 208.

²Jorgenson, Lloyd P., June 1963. "The Birth of a Tradition," *Phi Delta Kappan*, XLIV, No. 9, pp. 407-414.

³Freire, Paulo, 1970. *Pedagogy of the oppressed*. New York: Herder and Herder.

⁴Hoffer, Eric, 1951. *The true believer: thoughts on the nature of mass movements*. New York: Harper & Row Publishers.

Chapter Three

¹Seligman, Martin E. P., 1991. *Learned optimism*. New York: Alfred A. Knopf, p. 4.

²Seligman, p. 10.

³Tennen, Howard and Sharon Herzberger, 1985. "Attributional Style Questionnaire," *Test Critiques*, v. 4, pp. 20-30, Edited by D. J. Keyser and R. C. Sweetland. Kansas City: Test Corporation of America.

⁴Fraser, Steven (Editor), 1995. *The bell curve wars: race, intelligence, and the future of America*. New York: Basic Books.

⁵Myss, Caroline, 1996. *Anatomy of the spirit: the seven stages of power and healing*. New York: Harmony Books. pp. 209-213.

⁶Glasser, William, 1969. *Schools without failure*. New York: Harper & Row.

Chapter Four

¹Prigogine, Ilya and Isabelle Stengers, 1984. *Order out of chaos: man's new dialogue with nature*. New York: Bantam Books. p. 287.

²Prigogine, pp. 54-55.

[3]Blum, Harold F., 1962. *Time's arrow and evolution.* New York: Harper Torchbook.

[4]Blum, p. 15.

[5]Salk, Jonas Edward, 1973. *The survival of the wisest.* New York: Harper & Row, Publishers. pp. 7-30.

[6]McCrone, John, 1991. *The ape that spoke: language and the evolution of the human mind.* New York: William Morrow and Company, Inc. p. 26.

[7]McCrone, p. 174.

[8]United Nations, Department of International Economic and Social Affairs, 1992. *Long-range world population projections: two centuries of population growth: 1950-2150.* New York: United Nations.

[9]Heilbroner, Robert L., 1986. *The worldly philosophers: the lives, times, and ideas of the great economic thinkers.* New York: Touchstone Book. p. 78.

[10]Phillips, Kevin, 1990. *The politics of rich and poor: wealth and the American electorate in the Reagan aftermath.* New York: Random House. p. 88.

[11]Allport, Gordon W., 1979. *The nature of prejudice.* 25th Anniversary Edition. Reading, Massachusetts: Addison-Wesley Publishing Company. pp. 14-15.

[12]Exodus. Revised Standard Version.

[13]Martin, David L., February 1977. "Your Praise Can Smother Learning," *Learning.* pp. 45-48.

[14]Dreikurs, Rudolf and Loren Grey, 1968. *A new approach to discipline: logical consequences.* New York: Hawthorn Books, Inc. p. 56. Also see Dinkmeyer, Don C. and Rudolf Dreikurs, 1963. *Encouraging children to learn: the encouragement process.* Englewood Cliffs, NJ: Prentice-Hall, pp. 121 & 129.

[15]Seligman, Martin E. P., 1991. *Learned optimism.* New York: Alfred A. Knopf.

[16]Hoffer, Eric, 1951. *The true believer: thoughts on the nature of mass movements.* New York: Harper & Row Publishers.

Chapter Five

[1] Reisman, David, 1961. *The lonely crowd: a study of the changing American character.* New Haven: Yale University Press.

[2] Golding, William, 1955. *Lord of the flies.* New York: Capricorn Books.

[3] Golding, p. 189.

[4] Toepfer, Conrad F., April 10, 1980. "Brain Growth Periodization in Young Adolescents: Some Educational Implications." Presented at Annual Meeting of AERA, Boston, Mass: ERIC Document Number ED 187-175-TM-800-261.

[5] Epstein, H. T., 1978. "Growth Spurts during Brain Development: Implications for Educational Policy." In J. S. Cahall and A. F. Mirsky (Eds.) *Education and the brain.* Seventy-seventh Yearbook of the National Society for the Study of Education, 2, Chicago: University of Chicago Press.

[6] Peele, Stanton, 1981. *How much is too much: healthy habits or destructive addictions.* Englewood Cliffs, New Jersey: Prentice-Hall, Inc., pp. 5-6.

[7] Peele, p. 14.

[8] Peele, p. 29.

[9] Peele, p. 30.

[10] Peele, Stanton, 1989. *Diseasing of America: addiction treatment out of control.* Lexington, Mass.: Lexington Books.

[11] Peele, p. 238.

[12] Peele, p. 254.

[13] Peele, p. 255.

Chapter Six

[1] Muller, Robert, 1984. *New Genesis: shaping a global spirituality.* New York: Image Books.

[2] Muller, p. xvi.

[3] Muller, p. 22.

[4]Hutchins, Robert M., 1953. *The conflict in education in a democratic society.* New York: Harper and Row Publishers. Reprinted in 1972 by Greenwood Press.

[5]Strand, Ray D. MD. In the spring or late winter of 1983, Dr. Strand spoke to an adult group on the spiritual connection to healing and holistic medicine generally. This meeting was held at Westminster Presbyterian Church in Rapid City, South Dakota.

[6]Hutchins, p. 70.

[7]Williams, Redford and Virginia Williams, 1993. *Anger kills: seventeen strategies for controlling hostility that can harm your health.* New York: Times Books.

[8]Damasio, Antonio R., 1994. *Descartes' error: emotion, reason, and the human brain.* New York: Grosset/Putnam.

[9]Goleman, Daniel, 1995. *Emotional intelligence: why it can matter more than IQ.* New York: Bantam Books.

Chapter Seven

[1]Bettelheim, Bruno, November 1985. "Punishment Versus Discipline," *The Atlantic Monthly.* pp. 51-59.

[2]Dreikurs, Rudolf and Loren Grey, 1970. *A parents' guide to child discipline.* New York: Hawthorn Books, Inc., p. 22.

[3]Adler, Alfred, 1954, *Understanding human nature.* Greenwich, Connecticut: Fawcett Publications, Inc., pp. 28-29.

[4]Freire, Paulo, 1970. *Pedagogy of the oppressed.* New York: Herder and Herder.

[5]Gilliam, Judge Philip B, October, 1961. Judge Gilliam was a keynote speaker at the fall teachers convention of the Western region of South Dakota Education Association. The title of his address was "What's Wrong With People?" His topic was directed at questioning how intelligent a society is, that spends more per person to incarcerate its youth than to properly educate them. Incarceration rarely makes them productive and capable citizens.

[6]Kozol, Jonathon, 1991. *Savage inequalities: children in America's schools.* New York: Crown Publishers, Inc.

[7]Ryan, William, 1971. *Blaming the victim.* New York: Pantheon Books.

Chapter Eight

[1] Kübler-Ross, Elisabeth, 1969. *On death and dying: what the dying have to teach doctors, nurses, clergy, and their own families.* New York: Macmillan Publishing Company.

[2] Kübler-Ross, Elisabeth, 1975. *Death: the final stage of growth.* Englewood Cliffs, New Jersey: Prentice-Hall, Inc.

[3] Festinger, Leon, 1957. *A theory of cognitive dissonance.* Stanford, California: Stanford University Press, pp. 30-31.

[4] Kuhn, Thomas S., 1970. *The structure of scientific revolutions.* Chicago: The University of Chicago Press.

[5] Lee, Harper, 1960. *To kill a mockingbird.* Philadelphia: Lippincott. This book was made into the movie by the same title.

[6] Hutchins, Robert M., 1953. *The conflict in education in a democratic society.* New York: Harper and Row Publishers. Reprinted in 1972 by Greenwood Press.

[7] Collinge. William, 1996. *The American Holistic Health Association: complete guide to alternative medicine.* New York: Warner Books, Inc., p. 210.

[8] Fuller, R. Buckminster, 1981. *Critical path.* New York: St. Martin's Press.

[9] Fuller, pp. 7-8.

Chapter Nine

[1] Samples, Bob, 1981. *The mind of our mother: toward holonomy and planetary consciousness.* Reading, MA: Addison- Wesley Publishing Company, p. 43.

[2] Damasio, Antonio R., 1994. *Descartes' error: emotion, reason, and the human brain.* New York: Grosset/Putnam, pp. 249-250.

[3] Frankl, Viktor, E., 1992. Fourth Edition. *Man's search for meaning: an introduction to logotherapy.* Boston: Beacon Press., pp. 139-154.

[4] Henderson, Hazel, 1996. *Building a win/win world: life beyond global economic warfare.* San Franciso: Berrett-Koehler Publishers, p. 206.

[5] Seligman, Martin E. P., 1991. *Learned optimism.* New York: Alfred A. Knopf, pp. 4-5.

[6] Seligman, p. 5.

[7] Holst, Alvin W., April, 1994. *Assessment driven teacher education.* An unpublished report given at the Annual Spring Conference of the Nebraska Consortium for the Improvement of Teacher Education during the April 7-8 meeting at the University of Nebraska at Kearney, Kearney, Nebraska. The NCITE was formed in 1983 and included all thirteen institutions of higher education which prepare teachers in Nebraska. Copies of this report are available from the author.

[8] Greenleaf, Robert K., 1977. *Servant leadership: a journey into the nature of legitmate power and greateness.* Ramsey, New Jersey: Paulist Press.

[9] Ferguson, Marilyn, 1980. *The Aquarian conspiracy: personal and social transformation in the 1980's.* Los Angeles, CA: J. P. Tarcher, Inc., p. 276.

[10] Allport, Gordon W., 1979. *The nature of prejudice.* 25th Anniversary Edition. Reading, Massachusetts: Addison-Wesley Publishing Company. pp. 14-15.

[11] Allport, pp. 14-15.

[12] Harris, Thomas A., 1969, *I'm OK - You're OK: a practical guide to transactional analysis.* New York: Harper and Row, Publishers, Inc., p. 41.

[13] Dinkmeyer, Don and Lewis E. Losoncy, , 1980. *The encouragement book: becoming a positive person.* Englewood Cliffs, New Jersey: Prentice-Hall, Inc.

[14] Dinkmeyer, p. 61.

Chapter Ten

[1] Csikszentmihalyi, Mihaly, 1993. *The evolving self: a psychology for the third millennium.* New York: HarperCollins, Publishers, Inc. p. 120, the following is a direct quote.
"The term 'meme' was introduced about twenty years ago by the British biologist Richard Dawkins, who used it to describe a unit of cultural information comparable in its effects on society to those of the chemically coded instructions contained in the gene on the human organism."

[2] Berman, Morris, 1990. *Coming to our senses: body and spirit in the hidden history of the west.* New York: Bantam Books, pp. 221-252. The emphasis drawn upon here is the Copernican theory of heliocentricity which took on a life of its own in people like Galileo.

[3]Hemispheric Mode Indicator(HMI), 1993. Barrington, IL: EXCEL, Inc.

[4]Hunter, Madeline, October 1979. "Teaching is decision making." *Educational Leadership*, V. 37, No. 1, p. 63.

[5]Jung, Carl, 1976. *Psychological types*. New Jersey: Princeton University Press.

[6]McCarthy, Bernice, 1981. *The 4-MAT system: teaching to learning styles with right/left mode techniques*. Second Edition. Oak Brook, IL: Excel, Inc.

[7]McCarthy, p. 47.

[8]Kolb, David A., 1985. *LSI: learning-style inventory*. Boston: McBER and Company.

[9]Hunter, Madeline, February 1985. "What's wrong with Madeline Hunter?" *Educational Leadership*, V. 42, p. 58.

[10]O'Brien, Lynn, 1990. *The learning channel preference checklist - LCPC*. Rockville, MD: Specific Diagnostic Studies.

[11]Binet, Alfred, 1980. *The development of intelligence in children / by Alfred Binet and Theodore Simon; with marginal notes by Lewis M. Terman; new preface by Lloyd M. Dunn*. Nashville, TN: Williams Printing Company, p. 267. From *L'Amée Psych.*, 1911, pp. 145- 201 & 261.

[12]Jensen, Arthur A., 1979. "Outmoded theory or unconquered frontier?" *Creative Science and Technolology*, 2, pp. 16-29.

[13]Herrenstein, Richard J. and Charles Murray, 1994. *The bell curve: intelligence and class structure in American life*. New York: Free Press.

[14]Fraser, Steven, 1995, Editor. *The bell curve wars: race, intelligence, and the future of America*. New York: Basic Books.

[15]Travers, John F., 1970. *Fundamentals of education psychology*. Scranton, PA: Internatinal Textbook Company.

[16]Gardner, Howard, 1983. *Frames of mind: the theory of multiple intelligences*. New York: Basic Books.

[17]Sternberg, Robert J., 1988. *The triarchic mind: a new theory of human intelligence*. New York: Viking, pp. 535-206.

[18]Terman, Lewis M. and M. H. Oden, 1925. *The gifted group at midlife; thirty-five years' follow-up of the superior child, v. 5.* Stanford, CA: Stanford University Press, p. 152.

Chapter Eleven

[1]Herbert, Frank, 1990. *Dune.* New York: Ace Books. (1965)

[2]Stagner, Ross, October 1984. "PT Conversation with Frank Herbert - Master of Dune." *Psychology today,* p. 70.

[3]Stagner, p. 70.

[4]Evans, Bergen, 1968. *Dictionary of quotations.* New York: Delacorte Press, p. 231, #22.Livy [Titus Livius], 59 B.C.- A.D. 17. Roman historian. *Histories* XXXVIII . x/iv.

[5]Damasio, Antonio R., 1994. *Descartes' error: emotion, reason, and the human brain.* New York: Grosset/Putnam.

[6]Goleman, Daniel, 1995. *Emotional intelligence: why it can matter more than IQ.* New York: Bantam Books.

[7]Livy

[8]Goleman

[9]Damasio

[10]Glasser, William, 1969. *Schools without failure.* New York: Harper & Row.

[11]Glasser, William, 1986. *Control theory in the classroom.* New York: Harper & Row Publishers.

[12]Thoreau, Henry David, September 7, 1851. This statement was written in his personal journal. This citation comes from *Bartlet's Familiar Quotations,* Fifteenth and 125th Anniversary Edition, 1982. Boston: Little, Brown and Company.

[13]Roosevelt, Franklin Delano, March 4, 1933. This statement comes from his first inaugural address. This citation comes from *Bartlet's Familiar Quotations,* Fifteenth and 125th Anniversary Edition, 1982. Boston: Little, Brown and Company.

[14]Goleman, Daniel, 1995. *Emotional intelligence: why it can matter more than IQ.* New York: Bantam Books, p. 97.

[15]Goleman, Daniel, 1995. *Emotional intelligence: why it can matter more than IQ.* New York: Bantam Books, p. 34.

[16]Freire, Paulo, 1970. *Pedagogy of the oppressed.* New York: Herder and Herder.

[17]Williams, Redford and Virginia Williams, 1993. *Anger kills: seventeen strategies for controlling hostility that can harm your health.* New York: Times Books.

[18]Williams, pp. 4-14.

[19]Williams, pp.38-40.

Chapter Twelve

[1]Horace [Quintus Horatius Flaccus], 65-8 B.C. This statement was written in 23 B.C. *Odes, bk I..* This citation comes from *Bartlet's Familiar Quotations,* Fifteenth and 125th Anniversary Edition, 1982. Boston: Little, Brown and Company. p. 107, 13.

[2]Hawking, Stephen W., 1988. *A brief history of time: from the big bang to black holes.* New York: Bantam Books.

[3]Spitz, René, 1945. "Hospitalism," *The psychoanalytic study of the child,* V. 1. New York: International Universities Press, Inc., p. 72.

[4]Justice, Blair, 1987. *Who gets sick: how beliefs, moods, and thoughts affect your health.* Los Angeles: Jeremy P. Tarcher, Inc.

[5]Roth, Geneen, 1992. *When food is love: exploring the relationship between eating and intimacy.* New York: Plume.

[6]Roth, p. 18.

[7]Greene, Bob and Oprah Winfrey, 1996. *Make the connection: ten steps to a better life.* New York: Hyperion.

Chapter Thirteen

[1]Hutchins, Robert M., 1953. *The conflict in education in a democratic society.* New York: Harper and Row Publishers. Reprinted in 1972 by Greenwood Press.

[2]Bennett, William J., 1993. *The book of virtues: a treasury of great moral stories.* New York: Simon and Schuster.

[3]Hutchinson, Robert J., 1995. *The book of vices: a collection of classic immoral tales.* New York: Riverhead Books.

[4]Garrod, Andrew, 1993, Editor. *Approaches to moral development: new research and emerging themes.* New York: Teachers College, Columbia University, p. ix.

[5]Gilligan, Carol, 1982. *In a different voice: psychological theory and women's development.* Cambridge, MA: Harvard University Press.

[6]Rest, James R., 1986. *Moral development: advances in research and theory.* New York: Praeger, p. xiv.

[7]Rest, pp. 185-195.

[8]Rest, pp. 1-202.

[9]Rest, p. 177.

[10]Rest, p. 178.

[11]Holst, Alvin W. and Mary Martha Muck, March, 1994. *Assessing Ethical Development at the Undergraduate Level.* A report given at the fifth annual National Conference on Ethics in America, during the March 9-11 meeting at California State University, Long Beach. This report was published in the conference proceedings. Individual copies of this report are available from the primary author.

Chapter Fourteen

[1]Peck, M. Scott, 1978. *The road less traveled: a new psychology of love, traditional values and spiritual growth.* New York: A Touchstone Book.

[2]Peck, p. 81.

[3]Jampolsky, Gerald G., 1979. *Love is letting go of fear.* Millbrae, CA: Celestial Arts.

[4]Prigogine, Ilya and Isabelle Stengers, 1984. *Order out of chaos: man's new dialogue with nature.* New York: Bantam Books.

[5]Hutchins, Robert M., 1953. *The conflict in education in a democratic society.* New York: Harper and Row Publishers. Reprinted in 1972 by Greenwood Press.

[6]Campbell, Joseph, 1988. *The power of myth: with Bill Moyers.* Edited by Betty Sue Flowers. New York: Doubleday.

[7]Hillman, James, 1996. *The soul's code: in search of character and calling.* New York: Random House. p. 8.

[8]Myss, Caroline, 1996. *Anatomy of the spirit: the seven stages of power and healing.* New York: Harmony Books.

[9]Second Timothy, 4-14. Kings James translation.

[10]Moore, Thomas, 1994. *Soul mates: honoring mysteries of love and relationship.* New York: HarperCollins Books. pp. 261-262.

[11]Hillman, pp. 11-14.

Chapter Fifteen

[1]Dewey, John, 1939. *Freedom and culture.* New York: Capricorn Books.

[2]Dewey, pp. 127-128.

[3]Einstein, Albert. *The dictionary of thoughts: a cyclopedia of quotations,* 1965. Revision Editor, Ralph Emerson Browns. Standard Book Company, p. 588.

[4]Fromm, Erich, 1968. *Escape from freedom,* seventh printing. New York: Discus Books, pp. 37-38.

[5]Biddle, Francis B., 1951. *The fear of freedom.* Garden City, NY: Doubleday, p. 56.

[6]Nash, Paul, 1966. *Authority and freedom in education: an introduction to the philosophy of education.* New York: John Wiley & Sons, Inc., p. 63.

[7]Nash, p. 63-64.

[8]Nash, p. 64.

[9]Rogers, Carl R., 1983. *Freedom to learn for the 80's.* Columbus, OH: Charles E. Merrill Publishing Company.

[9]Rogers, p. 276.

Chapter Sixteen

[1]Kuhn, Thomas S., 1970. *The structure of scientific revolutions.* Chicago: The University of Chicago Press.

[2]Kuhn, p. 75.

[3]Kuhn, p. 77.

[4]Barker, Joel A., 1992. *Future edge: discovering the new paradigms of success.* William Morrow and Company, Inc., p. 140.

[5]Festinger, Leon, 1957. *A theory of cognitive dissonance.* Stanford, California: Stanford University Press.

[6]Festinger,

[7]MacIntyre, Alasdair, 1984. *After virtue.*, 2nd ed. Notre Dame, IN: University of Notre Dame Press.

[8]Gergen, David, March 17, 1997. "Editorial," *U.S. News and World Report,* p. 80, v. 22, No. 10.

[9]Holmes, Stephen, 1993. *The anatomy of antiliberalism.* Cambridge, MA: Harvard University Press, p. 5.

[10]Burns, James MacGregor, 1978. *Leadership.* New York: Harper and Row Publishers, p. 19.

Chapter Seventeen

[1]Nair, Keshavan, 1994. *A higher standard of leadership: lessons from the life of Gandhi.* San Franciso, CA: Berrett-Koehler Publishers.

[2]Maslow, Abraham H., 1954. *Motivation and personality.* Second Edition, New York: Harper and Row Publishers, p. 152.

[3]Erickson, Erik H., *Childhood and society,* Second Edition. New York: W. W. Norton.

[4]Sheehy, Gail, 1976. *Passages: predictable crises of adult life.* New York: E. P. Dutton.

[5]Erickson, Erik H., 1968. *Identity youth and crisis.* New York: W. W. Norton, p. 94.

[6]Sheehy, p. 28.

[7]Hawley, Gwen A., 1988. *Measures of psychosocial development(MPD).* Odessa, Florida: Psychological Assessment Resources, Inc.

[8]Thoreau, Henry David, 1854. *Walden.* This citation is taken from *The great books,* Chicago: The Great Books Foundation. First Year, Volume 8, Number 15. p, 33,

[9]Carter, Stephen L., 1996. *Integrity.* New York: Basic Books, p. 18.

[10]Kohn, Alfie, 1986. *No contest: the case against competition.* Boston: Houghton Mifflin Company.

[11]Kohn, p. 7.

[12]Kohn, p. 8.

[13]The National Commission on Excellence in Education, 1983. *A nation at risk: the imperative for educational reform: a report to the Nation and the Secretary of Education, United States Department of Education,* Terrell Bell, Secretary. Washington, D.C.: The Commission: (Supt. of Documents, U.S. G.P.O. distributor. This document was the cause of education being given a much higher priority in the American society than ever before.

[14]Kohn, p. 56.

[15]Kohn, p. 194.

[16]Freire, Paulo, 1970. *Pedagogy of the oppressed.* New York: Herder and Herder.

[17]Bernays, Edward L. The source of this information is from a NOVA video presentation, *The Image Makers,* A walk through the 20st century with Bill Moyers in which Moyers interviewed Mr. Bernays.

[18]Henderson, Hazel, 1996. *Building a win/win world: life beyond global economic warfare.* San Franciso: Berrett-Koehler Publishers, p. 58.

[19]Kozol, Jonathon, 1991. *Savage inequalities: children in America's schools.* New York: Crown Publishers, Inc.

[20]Carter, p. 18.

Chapter Eighteen

[1]Heilbronner, Robert L., 1986. *The worldly philosophers: the lives, times, and ideas of the great economic thinkers.* Sixth Edition. New York: A Touchstone Book, p. 78. Malthus wrote *An essay on the principle of population as it affects the future improvement of society* in 1798.

[2]Maslow, Abraham H., 1954. *Motivation and personality.* Second Edition, New York: Harper and Row Publishers, p. 164.

[3]James, William, 1943. *The varieties of religious experience.* New York: Modern Library.

4Csikszentmihalyi, Mihaly, 1990. *Flow: the psychology of optimal experience*. New York: Harper Perennial, p. 39.

5The National Commission on Excellence in Education, 1983. *A nation at risk: the imperative for educational reform: a report to the Nation and the Secretary of Education, United States Department of Education*, Terrell Bell, Secretary. Washington, D.C.: The Commission: (Supt. of Documents, U.S. G.P.O. distributor. This document was the cause of education being given a much higher priority in the American society than ever before.

6Einsten, Albert. 1879-1955. This statement is attributed to Einstein. The Institute for Advanced Study, in Princeton, New Jersey, where Einstein taught, is unable to find when he said this, in what publication it is recorded, and the context in which he said it. The only source of the quote they found was at a web site at Stanford University on Einstein's quotes. This source provided no background on the quote.

7A career as an educator was largely a short term experience for adolescent, unwed females, until 1945 when the G. I. Bill made it possible for returning service personnel to go to college. Many of these people were men as well as women. These people began lifetime careers in education in the late forties and early fifties as the first generation of career educators. This represents a forty year time span in education and most of these are retiring or preparing to retire. The second generation of career educators are now beginning to fill the ranks of professional educators.

8Haeckel, Ernst Heinrich. 1868. This statement was written in *The history of creation*. This citation comes from *Bartlet's Familiar Quotations*, Fifteenth and 125th Anniversary Edition, 1982. Boston: Little, Brown and Company, p. 617, 10.

Epilogue

[1]Shannon, George, 1992. *A knock at the door, the Oryx multiculural folktale series.* Phoenix, AZ: Oryx Press, pp. 148-152. Folktales are continually told and retold. Most of them have been altered by the story teller for various reasons. The original story is then usually diluted and the intended moral is not conveyed in metaphor.

The parallel used as the epilogue was a story told to me as a child. However I was not able to find the exact story, in written form, which I was told. The major variation is the Three Little Pigs being reunited when the Wolf is boiled and his belly opened by the last little pig. There are other stories of female goats opening the belly of the Wolf with a sharp hoof or horn and recovering the "kids". I trust the reader will read the epilogue and be able to identify the intended meaning.

INDEX

Aadams, J., 217

acceptance, 106, 113

Acton, Lord, 145

addiction, 14, 36,,63
 a solution, 65
 a means of controlling fear, 70

Adler, A., 73, 85, 127

Adlerian Psychology, 60

advantage, 196-199

Age of Compassion, 115, 124

Age of Games, 51, 53, 124, 228

Age of War, 51, 52, 124

Agnew, S., 171

Agricultural Age, 51, 52

alienation, 63

Allport, G., 56, 117, 121

American Psychological
 Association, 141

American Revolution, 210

American Tobacco
 Company, 229

anger, 155

anorexia, 167

anti-liberalism, 211

Applewhite, M., 176

Aristotle, 44, 147, 170-172

Arizona State University,
 140, 241

"at risk", 82

Attributional Style
 Questionnaire (ASQ), 33

Barker, J., 205

baseball, 53

basketball, 53

Bear Butte, SD, 96

behaviorism, 60

bell-shaped curve, 34, 35

Bennett, W. 170

Berman, M., 129

Bernays, E. L., 229

Bettelheim, B., 85

Biddle, F. B., 200

Binet, A., 140, 141

biofeedback, 164

Black Hills, SD, 96

blaming, 89

Blum, H. F., 44

brain growth spurts, 68

Branch Davidians, 78, 176

Brooks, V. W., 73

bulimia, 167

Burns, G. M., 212

Buzon, T., 7

Camp David Accords, 55

Campbell, J., 26, 184

Carter, Pres. J., 55

Carter, S., 220, 234

Cary, J., 127

categorical imperative, 171, 176

Chadron State College, 175

chaos, 43, 182, 237, 239, 244
 a state of mind, 4

Christianity, 214

268 INDEX

civil disobedience, 214

Civil War, 53.

closed system, 43, 56, 192, 193, 200, 206, 209, 210, 213, 222, 223, 226, 234, 242
  culture of, 243
  a means of control, 45
  diagram, 51

cognitive dissonance, 91, 100, 206

Cold War, 28

collaboration, 230

commitment, 231

Communism, the Devil, 28

competition, 34, 222, 223

consensus, 231

conservative, 209

consumerism, 188

contract, 228

control of others, 33

cooperation, 226, 227

cooperative learning, 226

Copernicus, 44

corruption, 145-148

critical mass, 204, 246

Csikszentmihaly, M., 240

cult, 176, 201, 214, 222

daimon, 185

DARE, 67

Das, Baba Ram, 129

Defining Issues Test (DIT), 173

Demasio, A., 79

Descartes, R., 79, 103, 147, 149

despair, 219

Dewey, J., 196

dieting, 167

Dinkmeyer, D., 124

discipline, 84, 115, 116, 123, 192, 244

divine command, 171

divorce, 228

Djilas, M., 73

Doubleday, Gen., 53

Dreikurs, R., 60, 85

Drieser, T., 191

drug, problem, 13, 21

dualism, tame vs. wild, 36, 110

dysfunctional
  defifintion, 25
  contributors, 30-32
  cultural, 43

economics, 222, 223, 232

education, early, 20

Einstein, A., 21, 199, 217, 243

Eisenhauer, Pres, D. D., 112

emotional power, 145-157

encouragement, 115, 116, 121, 124, 192, 244

energy components, 76

engineered consent, 229

entropy, 45

Epstein, H. T., 68

Eriskson, E., 217

ethical egoism, 176

ethical power, 169-180

ethics, 23

Evers, M., 95

Exodus 21:23-25, 59
fanatic, 29, 201
fanaticism, 61, 199
fear, 15, 39, 146-148, 238
fear as a symptom, 15, 163, 181, 182
Ferguson, M., 115
Festinger, L., 91, 92, 206
Feurstein, 7
Fitzgerald, Z. S., 11
flow, 240
folkways, 27
football, 53
Ford, Pres. G., 225
Frankl, V., 103
free enterprise, 233
freedom, 193, 196
freedom, defined, 201
Freire, P., 6, 28, 87, 154, 229
Fromm, E., 200
Fuller, R. B., 100
Galileo, 46, 92, 93, 97
games, 53
Gandhi, Mahatma, 191, 214, 215
gangs, 66
Gardner, H., 7, 141
gene, 129, 222, 246
genetic
  coding, 21
  DNA, 18
  messages, 18, 19
gifted programs, 143
Gilliam, Judge, 88

Gilligan, C., 172
Glasser, W., 39, 150
"going back to zero rule," 205
Golding, W., 65, 66
Goleman, D., 79, 147, 148, 152
grade inflation, 35
Greene, B., 168
Greenleaf, R., 107, 191
guilt, 39, 64, 71, 153, 182
Gutenberg, 130
Haeckel, E. H., 246
Harris, T., 121
Harvard, 141
hate, 28, 29, 60, 61, 151, 199, 211
Hawking, S., 161
Hawley, G., 218
Heaven's Gate, 176, 223
heliocentric, 46, 92
hemispheric mode indicatior (HMI), 133
Henderson, H., 105, 232
Herbert, F., 145
heresy, 28, 46, 92
hero, 19
Herrnstein, R. J., 141
Hillman, J., 185
Hoffer, Eric, 29, 60, 127, 211
holistic medicine, 8, 78, 97
Holmes, S., 211
hope, 106, 113
Horace, 160

INDEX

Hungarian revolt, 110

Hunter, M., 134, 138

Hutchins, R., 7, 77, 97, 169, 184

Hutchinson, R., 172

Huxley, A., 217

ignorance, 14, 15, 146, 199, 202
  basis of hate, 29

independence, 230

indoctrination, 223

Industrial/Technological Age, 51, 52

Information/Service Age, 116, 124

inner-directed, 18

integrity, 81, 213, 219, 220, 237-246
  exemplars of, 213-235
  model of, 76, 91, 98

intellectual power, 129-144

intelligence quotient (IQ), 140
  group test, 141
  multiple, theory of, 142

inter-dependence, 234

isomers, 238

ITIP, 138

James, W., 217, 240

Jampolsky, J., 181, 184

Jefferson, T., 191, 217, 242

Jensen, A., 140

Jesus Christ, 130, 214

Johnson, Pres. L. B., 55, 225

joy, 238-240

Jung, C. G., 73, 136

Justice, Blair, 163

Kant, I., 5, 171

Kennedy, Pres. J., 207

Kennedy, R., 207

King James Bible, 188

King, Rev. M. L., Jr., 207, 215

Kohlberg, L., 172, 175, 179

Kohn, A., 225

Koresh, D., 176

Korologos, T., 207

Kozol, J., 89, 233

Kübler-Ross, E., 91

Kuhn, T., 92, 203

Lakota, 52

lazy, defined, 188

leadership, 198, 212
  servant, 107

learning
  difficulty, 68
  left brain, 68, 134
  modality, 138
  plateaus, 68
  right brain, 68 134
  style, 136
  trial and error, 25, 26

Learning Channels Preference Checklist (LCPC), 139

Learning Style Inventory (LSI), 137

legal action, 222

liberal, 209, 211

liberty, 193, 196

life, 183
  defined, 15
  meaning, 15
  unexamined, 25

Lincoln, A., 208, 217

litigation, 227

Livy, 146

Lorge-Thorndike IQ Test, 141

Loscocy, L., 124

Lott, T., 208

love, 115, 116, 183, 192, 244
 definition, 117, 181, 182
 steps of, 117-121

MacIntyre, A., 207

Malthus, T. R., 50, 237

market domination, 224

marriage, 222, 232

Maslow, A., 216

Maughm, W. M., 127

McCarthy, B., 7, 136

McCullogh, C., 11

Measure of Pyshosocial Development (MPD), 218

meme, 129, 141, 222, 246

Meredith, J., 3, 94

mid-life crisis, 218

Mills, F., 241

Mississippi, University of, 93, 208
 Ole Miss, 94, 179

modality, 138

Moore, T., 188, 189

moral development, 220, 221

moral power, 169-180

morals, 23

mores, 27

Moscow, seat of evil, 30

Moyers, W., 26

Muller, R., 7, 75, 76

Murray, C., 140

Muskie, E., 149

Myss, C., 37, 186

mystic experience, 240

myths, 26, 28, 184, 185

NAACP, 95

Nash, P., 201

Nation At Risk, The, 225, 243

National Ethics Conference, 175

National Science Foundation, 3, 93

Natrona County
 Court House, 95
 High School, 95

negotiation, 227

Newton, Sir I., 44

Newtonian laws, 182

Nixon, Pres. R. M., 55, 145, 171

normal distribution, 35

nomad, 222
 way of life, 49
 replacement, 50, 51

non-violence, 214

Oorlog, Coach H., 240

open system, 43, 103, 116, 192, 196, 213, 231, 234, 244-246

optimism
 definition, 105
 effect upon health, 105
 teaching of, 107

pain, 13, 238

paradigm, 92, 211

paradigm shift, 203-212

passage, 218

peak experience, 240

Peck, M. S., 181

Peele, S., 69, 70

pessimism, 31

pessimist, definition, 33

physical power, 159-168

Plato, 11, 23, 133, 134

point of inflection, 49, 54, 56

politikos, 206

population growth curve, 46, 47, 116

Postman, N., 6

power
  win/lose, 34, 56, 109, 114
  win/win, 104, 108 112, 114, 116

praise, 59, 60, 115, 192, 243

prejudice, 56, 104, 115, 192, 211, 216, 243
  steps of, 57-59

Prigogine, I., 44, 182

Profile of Nonverbal Sensitivity, (PONS), 152

Protestant schools, 27

Psychology Today, 146

psychological position, 222

punishment, 59, 115, 123, 149, 192, 223, 243

punishment, 85
  used as discipline, 87

Puritans, 27, 200

Quakers, 27

Parks, Rosa, 150

rationality, 21

Reagan, N., 67

Reagan, Pres. R., 30, 55, 225

Reality Therapy, 150

Reconstruction Era, 208

Reeb, Rev., 95

Reisman, D., 18, 64

religion, 222

Rest, J., 173

Rico, G., 7

Rogers, C., 201

Roman Catholic Church, 28, 212

Roosevelt, E., 217

Roosevelt, Pres. F. D., 152, 207

Rosenthal, R., 152

Roth, G., 167, 168

Rowe, M. B., 60

Ryan, W., 89

Salk, J., 46, 49, 56

Samples, R. 103

Santayana, G., 11

scarcity, 34

schools
  Prostestant, 27
  public, 27

Scott, E. 127

secrecy, 38

sect, 227

self-actualizing, 216

Seligman, M., 31, 105

Seneca, L. A., 73

shame, 39, 152, 238

Sheehy, G., 217

sigmoid curve, 46-48, 116, 175, 222, 227

sin, seven deadly, 170

slavery, 27, 208

Socrates, 132

soul, 183-186, 191, 244

Spencer, H., 191

Spinoza, 217

spiritual power, 181-189

spirituality, 183

Spitz, R., 162

Sternberg, R., 142

Strand, R., 8, 77, 78

submission, 229

taboo, 27

Tarrytown, NY, 7, 141

tautomeric balance, 238

Terman, L. M., 142

terror, 39, 64, 71, 182

theory, definition, 96

thermodynamics, 44
    second law, 45

Thoreau, H.D., 15, 18, 151, 214, 219

Thorndike, E. L., 141

time as an invention, 23

Toepfer, C. F., 68

Transactional Analysis (TA), 121, 223, 232

treason, 28

Twain, Mark, 95

tyranny, 197

United Nations, Dept. of International Economic & Social Affairs, 49

universal ethical principles, 179

vice, 169, 239, 240

victimization, 186-188

virtue, 169, 239, 240

virtus, 170

vitium, 170

volunteerism, 233

Waco, TX, 176

War
    age of, 51, 52
    Vietnam, 54, 55
    World War II, 54

Washington, D. C., 53

Watergate Building, 171

weakness
    seen as a defect, 36
    strengths seen as weakness, 37

wealth
    food, 51
    human, 116, 125
    matter & energy, 51

Weingartner, C., 6

wholeness, 220

Wilkins, R., 95

Williams, R. & V., 78, 156

Winfrey, O., 168

Wounded Knee, SD
    massacre, 52

woundedness, 232

Yale, 141

Young Citizen's League (YCL), 188

Yugoslavia, 162

To order additional copies of *Integrity, Courage, & Soul* use this form or a photocopy.

Ship to: (please print)

Name_____

Address_____

City, State, Zip_____

Day phone_____

_____copies of *Integrity, Courage, & Soul*
@$17.95 each _____
Postage and handling
@$4.50 perbook_____
South Dakota residents
add 4% state sales tax_____

Total amount enclosed_____

Make checks payable to **Alvin W. Holst**

**Send to: Alvin W. Holst
3023 Tomahawk Drive
Rapid City, SD 57702**